Praise for *Making a Difference by Being Yourself*

"Provides commonsense yet insightful examples of ways to connect people to others and to their workplace. I'm excited about sharing Huszczo's observations with my colleagues and urge you to 'catch the fever' and read this book."

—JACK P. NIGHTINGALE, ASSISTANT DIRECTOR OF HIGHER EDUCATION
ORGANIZING, AMERICAN FEDERATION OF TEACHERS

"Huszczo is an expert on the application of personality type to daily life and a man who makes a difference. His book is a simple and effective presentation of how anyone can use his or her core functions to make a difference, too."

—JOHN W. LORD, EXECUTIVE DIRECTOR,
THE ASSOCIATION FOR PSYCHOLOGICAL TYPE INTERNATIONAL

"Finally, a book grounded in research that matches personal narrative to personality type. It opens new fields of investigation while expanding the range of tools available to the consultant. This book is a must-read."

—TONY PICCHIONI, PHD, CHAIR, DEPARTMENT OF HUMAN DEVELOPMENT,
ANNETTE CALDWELL SIMMONS SCHOOL OF EDUCATION AND HUMAN
DEVELOPMENT, SOUTHERN METHODIST UNIVERSITY

"Identifies critical features of how each of us can make a difference at work, at home, at play, or in our community simply by recognizing our personality type. This provides a more inclusive alternative to 'getting the right people on the bus' to achieve a particular goal."

—FRANK C. BROSIUS, MD,
PROFESSOR AND CHIEF OF THE DIVISION OF KIDNEY DISEASES,
UNIVERSITY OF MICHIGAN

"A brilliant synthesis of research and pragmatic, action-oriented insights that individuals can use for personal development or the development of their clients. From the opening words to the last page, this book will deepen your use of psychological type."
—ROGER R. PEARMAN, EDD, PRESIDENT, QUALIFYING.ORG®, INC.

"A practical approach to knowing and using who we are to more effectively interact with those we come into contact with on a daily basis to make a difference in our lives."
—DARYLL MCCARTHY, ADMINISTRATIVE SUPPORT SUPERVISOR, HUMAN RESOURCE DEPARTMENT, CITY OF PLANO, TEXAS

"Describes the clearest way you can stand in your own force by just being you. Enjoy, learn, use that knowledge! Huszczo's work will truly make a difference in your life, too!"
—LIEVE VERMEULEN, PRESIDENT, TYPE ASSOCIATION BENELUX

"Huszczo's easy style and poignant stories help you realize how true-to-type, positive, ordinary acts can have a profound impact on your work and your relationships. I challenge anyone to read this book and walk away unmoved, untouched, and unmotivated to act."
—VICTORIA A. HOEVEMEYER, ORGANIZATIONAL DEVELOPMENT DIRECTOR, FRIENDSHIP VILLAGE OF SCHAUMBURG, SCHAUMBURG, ILLINOIS

"Huszczo's research can help us transform our MBTI® personality profile from a statement of who we are to a plan for how we can make a difference. His case studies offer realistic, day-to-day ways each of us can make a difference by doing what comes naturally."
—BRAD HILL, PRINCIPAL, TANDEHILL HUMAN CAPITAL

"Huszczo's extensive research and background with the MBTI assessment will make this book insightful for even the most experienced user. Huszczo has a great ability to develop practical tools for everyday applications and illustrate their use with personal experiences."
—TED AMSDEN, SENIOR CONSULTANT, THE LEADERSHIP GROUP LLC

"Takes a fresh approach to using personality type to enhance your ability to make impactful differences, no matter what stage in life you're at."
—GRETCHEN E. BENSCH, COORDINATOR, HUMAN RESOURCE GENERALIST, PMA CONSULTANTS

"Huszczo gets it when it comes to using the MBTI tool to help solve problems. I am anxious to use his latest research to assist clients seeking to integrate life and work. It will make a difference."
—MARILYN L. TAYLOR, MS, PRESIDENT, TAYLOR TRAINING & DEVELOPMENT INC.

"Huszczo brings decades of MBTI experience to this practical guide. His exercises can help people identify and develop their natural strengths. This book would be helpful to anyone who wants to be authentic as well as successful."
—NANCY SCHULLERY, PHD, PROFESSOR, BUSINESS INFORMATION SYSTEMS, AND DIRECTOR OF UNDERGRADUATE PROGRAMS, HAWORTH COLLEGE OF BUSINESS, WESTERN MICHIGAN UNIVERSITY

"Huszczo focuses the spotlight inward as we learn how to enrich our lives and the lives of others by using our special gifts and allowing our personalities to shine through."
—JIM MCNEIL, CHANGE CONSULTANT, STRATEM ASSOCIATES/COMPETITIVE DYNAMICS INTERNATIONAL

"If everyone could feel that they can make a difference, that they can make a valid contribution to their workplace, their relationships, and their community simply by being who they are naturally, it would change the world."
—MARILYN MAXIM, MANAGER, PUBLIC RELATIONS, KEILHAUER

"Recognizing my natural personality preferences has made me a better business partner, a better parent, and a more active partner in my community. This process has contributed to an improved value in my involvement with others in my life."
—JULIE LYNCH, NSK AMERICAS, MANAGER, BENEFITS

Making a Difference
by Being Yourself

Making a Difference

by Being Yourself

Using Your Personality Type to Find Your Life's True Purpose

GREGORY E. HUSZCZO

NICHOLAS BREALEY
PUBLISHING

BOSTON · LONDON

This edition first published by Nicholas Brealey Publishing in 2010. Original hard-cover edition first published by Davies-Black in 2008:

20 Park Plaza, Suite 1115A
Boston, MA 02116, USA
Tel: 617-523-3801
Fax: 617-523-3708

3-5 Spafield Street, Clerkenwell
London, EC1R 4QB, UK
Tel: +44-(0)-207-239-0360
Fax: +44-(0)-207-239-0370

www.nicholasbrealey.com

Printed in the United States of America

14 13 12 11 10   1 2 3 4 5

ISBN: 978-1-85788-547-7

The Library of Congress has previously catalogued this edition as follows:
Huszczo, Gregory E.
    Making a difference by being yourself : using your personality type to find your
    life's true purpose / Gregory E. Huszczo.
        p. cm.
    Includes bibliographical references and index.
    ISBN: 978-0-89106-223-3
    1. Personality and occupation. 2. Employees—Psychology.
    3. Employees—Attitude. 4. Performance.
    5. Personality assessment. I. Title.
BF698.9.O3H87 2008
155.2'6—dc22
                                                            2008015767

FIRST EDITION
First printing 2008

To Dr. Cecil Williams,

*a man who made a big difference in my life
and in the lives of so many others*

CONTENTS

PREFACE

Interest in stories about people making a difference has never been higher. If you do an internet search for the phrase, *make a difference,* you will be referred to more than twenty-six million sites. Hundreds of companies advertise their products or services in a manner that emphasizes how they make a difference. The tag line "making a difference" is utilized in volunteer recruitment by the majority of non profit agencies that offer help to communities. *USA Weekend* magazine continues to sponsor Make a Difference Day every October and now offers cash awards for worthy projects. Oprah Winfrey has launched "Oprah's Angel Network" to encourage people to donate, volunteer, and get involved. A "Making a Difference Network" exists to facilitate the granting of wishes to people in very difficult circumstances. *NBC Nightly News with Brian Williams* broadcasts a weekly "Making a Difference" segment on profiles of ordinary people doing extraordinary things.

This book has contributed to the movement by helping people realize that making a difference is something we all can do on a very regular basis. It is about ordinary people doing what is ordinary to them—being themselves. Since *Making a Difference by Being Yourself* was first published in its hardcover edition in October of 2008, I have received several hundred more stories of people making a difference. I have heard from readers that this book helped them make a difference at their place of work, in their relationships, and in their communities.

What if I told you that the key to making a difference boils down to you truly being yourself? This may sound simple, but it won't always be easy. In order for you to be yourself, you must become aware of the elements of your core personality. In order to make a difference, you need the courage to use your personality. Socrates said, "The unexamined life is not worth living." This book helps you examine yourself without judgment, and then urges you to go beyond being self-aware and to consider your uses in life. *Making a Difference by Being Yourself* will move you to take action by being you—not by being a superhero or by trying to be all things to all people, but by doing things consistent with who you are. I can assure you, if you are willing to consciously act on the essence of who you are, you will make a difference.

In order to produce this book, I conducted three research studies in which more than five hundred people told me stories about times they made a difference. I have included over a hundred of these stories throughout the pages of this book in order to give you ideas about how your personality type might make a difference. Any good story has a lot to teach us. This is not a book about extraordinary people doing extraordinary things. You will not be hearing about the Warren Buffets or the Abraham Lincolns of the world making a difference through amazing deeds. This book is about ordinary people who simply want to make more of a difference for themselves and for the people and organizations they care about. Most of the stories are about everyday life experiences (for example, helping an overwhelmed friend produce a step-by-step to-do list), because making small differences frequently adds up to a life of happiness and fulfillment. Says children's rights advocate Marian Wright Edelman, "We must not, in trying to think about how we can make a big difference, ignore the small daily differences we can make which, over time, add up to big differences that we often cannot foresee."

Some of the stories are kind of wild—for example, a college student protecting her girlfriend from being written on with magic markers after she had passed out at a party. Many of the stories will provide insights on how people made a difference at work by being themselves. And some of the stories are as heartwarming as the one below.

"I worked for a year as an educational assistant in a special education classroom. I made the point of getting to know each student personally. Kids would come to me when they were having trouble at home or school. I did something special for each kid on their birthday. I also popped in on them during lunch. I sent notes to them about how much I enjoyed talking with them. I made a point of visiting one of 'my girls' when she was admitted to a psych ward. I also bonded with the full-time teacher assigned to the class. I brought her flowers on the anniversary of her brother's suicide and took over the class that day so she could have private time to herself."

All five hundred people in my research studies were able to tell me stories about times they made a difference. Some needed encouragement to share their stories, but all of them made a difference in the arenas of work and relationships. In addition, virtually everyone reported that making a difference in one arena enhanced their ability to make a difference in another. They also admitted that making a difference for others made a big difference for themselves. It made them feel happier and more fulfilled. Making a difference is a fundamental need, and probably a universal experience. Being yourself is a key to experiencing a sense of well-being. I hope you will be willing to post *your* stories on my website (makingadifference type.com) and on my Facebook page (Making a Difference).

Throughout this book, you will learn how different personalities make a difference, differently. You will be guided into understanding the typical strengths of your core personality through simple self-assessment instruments and exercises. Once you understand the fundamentals of your personality type, you will be prepared to increase the frequency with which you will make a difference. This book is about you, not about the subjects of my research studies. You won't be asked to look too deeply into your personality, but you will be asked to identify four tendencies in your style. And you will be pushed to *use* the information about yourself to find opportunities to make a difference.

Part One of this book is for everyone. Chapters 1–3 introduce you to the topics of positive psychology, making a difference, living life consciously, and discovering your core personality type. Some sections of Part Two are just for you. Chapters 4–7 focus on the four core personality types and one of those chapters will be particularly useful to you at work and in your relationships. Throughout the book you will find forms and exercises to enhance your ability to make a difference. Chapter 8 will help you pull it all together. However, reading a book is not enough—you must personalize what you learn and put it to use. The goal is to make "making a difference" something that comes naturally to you. Join the movement. Make a difference by being yourself!

ACKNOWLEDGMENTS

I am exceedingly grateful to the more than five hundred people who were willing to share with me their stories about times when they had made a difference, and who made the time to fill out questionnaires. These are the people who provided the substance for this book.

I also want to thank my team of graduate students. Particular thanks go to Rick Opland and Gretchen Bensch, who coauthored papers with me. A big thank-you goes out to Brian Walton and Pacquale Caruso, Rebecca Clark deCastillo, Kascia Czajka, Freida Edoh-Bedi, Maher Jafar, Crosby Houpt, Chen Xingzhi, and Ari Black for entering mounds of data so I could focus on the analyses. Carrol Muglia and Janan Daniels, who typed up the more than fifteen hundred stories I received, made things a lot easier for me.

This book was brought to fruition by the wonderful staff at Davies-Black Publishing. Connie Kallback, senior acquisitions editor, started the process, but Laura Lawson, who has since taken over the position, has been particularly helpful. She went over a mountain of material, cajoled me into meeting deadlines, and helped with the structure of the book. Mark Chambers provided much-needed help with the copyediting. Lee Langhammer Law, vice president and publisher, has always been encouraging throughout my relationship with Davies-Black. Laura Simonds, director of marketing and sales, has been helpful in promoting my previous books and has great plans for promoting this one.

I have been blessed to have some terrific people make a difference in my work life. My mentors—Cecil Williams, Carl Frost, Don Ephlin, and Neal Schmitt—have taught me so much and helped launch and develop my career as an industrial-organizational psychologist. I am grateful to my colleagues in the master's of science in human resources and organizational development (MSHROD) program at Eastern Michigan University for emphasizing the importance of collaboration and support. The organizational clients I have been able to work with in my consulting practice have taught me volumes about the ups and downs of life at work in the real world. It was an honor to be able to observe them as they made a difference in a wide variety of organizational settings.

This book has benefited from the pioneers in the positive psychology movement. The research generated by them has been inspirational. Their notion that we should look at what is good with us and not just what our problems are has made a difference for me. I am also grateful to the Association for Psychological Type International (APTi) community for continuing to further the work of Carl Jung, Isabel Myers, and Katharine Briggs, whose frameworks and theories are really the seminal works of the positive psychology movement. I especially want to thank the Hirsh family (Sandra, Katherine, and Elizabeth) for their encouragement and support.

My biggest thank-you goes to my wife, Kathy, for making such a huge difference in my relationship life. She has always been there for me, encouraging me and making sure life is fun. Our kids, Sam and Anne, have been a joy to watch blossom into adulthood. I am grateful that my brother Mike and sister-in-law Jan are such great teammates and help in so many family matters. I am glad that my mother, Virginia, still shows her sense of humor. She and my father, Edward, taught me the importance of making a difference at work and in relationships in a very fundamental way.

Making a Difference
and Discovering
Who You Are

Why Is Making a Difference So Important?

It's easy to make a buck. It's a lot tougher to make a difference.
—TOM BROKAW

There is growing evidence that the key to success in work organizations is to have people focus on their strengths. The positive psychology movement declares that the key to people's mental and physical health is their figuring out what is right with themselves, not focusing on their neuroses, psychoses, and shortcomings. Do you know what is right with you? Can you describe your natural tendencies, and are you ready to make a difference with those tendencies?

The funny thing, it turns out, is that all you really have to do to make a difference is be yourself. That said, do you know who you are? This book will help you identify key elements of your personality—but more important, it will help you use your personality. Millions of people every year attend workshops and take assessments to discover their personality type and maybe learn about the personalities of their coworkers. But, sadly, most fail to utilize the valuable insights they've gained in the process.

HOW IMPORTANT IS MAKING A DIFFERENCE IN TODAY'S WORLD?

If you do a Google search for "make [or making] a difference," you will identify literally millions of sites that reference this topic. Many communities have established "Making a Difference" days, when people can volunteer to help those in need. In fact, the people at *USA Weekend* magazine have attempted to turn this into a national event. They have declared the fourth Saturday of every October Make A Difference Day. In one weekend alone, over three million people volunteered and accomplished thousands of projects in hundreds of towns. *USA Weekend* has also established a Web site with examples of projects completed and ideas for additional projects and suggestions on how to get involved to organize others.

The opportunity to make a difference motivates people. Service agencies such as AmeriCorps and the Peace Corps recruit people by pointing out that they can fulfill their need to make a difference by becoming more involved in their work and mission. The theme is used in advertising campaigns for charitable foundations. Service America and many other organizations use it as a slogan. Making a difference is offered as the motivation for service trips for college students (as an alternative to spring break), awards for teachers, and opportunities to develop one's leadership skills. Web sites such as bethecause.org, cityyear.org, and go-mad.org help people find opportunities for making a difference.

The entertainment industry has also trumpeted the notion. Popular movies such as *It's a Wonderful Life* and *Pay It Forward* depict heartwarming stories that show ordinary people doing things that make a difference in their job, in their community, and for their families, friends, coworkers, and even strangers. Several news programs have used it as a theme. For example, the *NBC Nightly News* with Brian Williams dedicated a segment every week to stories about people making a difference.

Many best-selling nonfiction books have described the benefits of doing things for the benefit of others. Robert Greenleaf's classic *Servant Leadership* (1977) espouses making a difference as a leader by focusing on what followers need to succeed. Mihály Csikszentmihályi's best-selling work *Flow* (1990) examines the psychology of peak experiences and shows that happiness comes from delivering our best by being focused and challenged to make a difference for ourselves and others. In *The Tipping Point* (2000), Malcolm Gladwell presents compelling evidence for how making small differences can make a big difference in work and in efforts to change the society at large. Tal Ben-Shahar, who leads a wildly popular positive psychology seminar at Harvard University, identifies in his book *Happier* (2007) the key principles for becoming happier; most of these lead back to making a difference and living life consciously. Clearly the topic of making a difference has inspired millions of people in this country and throughout the world.

WHY IS MAKING A DIFFERENCE SO IMPORTANT TO US?

Feeling like you make a difference in the world is a basic human desire. It fulfills several needs, including the need to feel there is meaning to one's life, a sense of significance. Henry Thoreau presented the bleak perspective that most people "live lives of quiet desperation." Yet, virtually all people have peak moments; we just need to prompt them to pay attention to those moments and dedicate themselves to having them more often. When I asked the five hundred people in my research studies to relay stories of times when they had made a difference, all were able to point to examples. Ben-Shahar, who makes a compelling case for the ultimate importance of happiness, defines happiness as the times when we experience both pleasure and meaning in our lives. The United States of America was founded on the basic right of the pursuit of happiness. When we make a difference for ourselves or for others, we find meaning in life and feel happier—whether at work or in our relationships. Ralph Waldo Emerson pointed out that "It is one of the most beautiful compensations of this life that no man can sincerely try to help another without helping himself."

MAKING A DIFFERENCE AS AN ALTERNATIVE TO PERFECTIONISM

Are you prone to perfectionism? Are you more likely to point out what is lacking in a situation or effort than what is there? Do you discount your efforts when you are praised at work, or by loved ones or neighbors? This book urges you to focus on whether things got better rather than worse, instead of whether what you or others did was perfect. The concept of making a difference provides a healthy alternative to perfectionism. Psychotherapists such as Karen Horney have documented the negative impact of the "curse of perfectionism" and the "tyranny of the should." These tendencies often inhibit us from even trying to make a difference and later from feeling the satisfaction of helping ourselves and others.

Making a difference can be both exhilarating and humbling. It encourages us to be human, not godlike, while still exerting the effort to engage in something challenging. The standard of "making a difference"—that is, making things better—provides the pathway for avoiding the temptation to think we need to be perfect yet still not abandoning our standards to the point that "anything goes" or "nothing matters." Considerable evidence—from both research and experience—suggests that small things make a big difference both to ourselves and to others in our life. If we can allow ourselves to feel happy about the little ways we make a difference, we can actually broaden our scope of attention and be less prone to be self-absorbed. Research by Isen, Clark, and Schwartz (1976) and George (1991) confirms that we are more likely to help others when we feel good. Are you willing to let go of some perfectionistic tendencies and feel good about being you? Are you willing to allow yourself the pleasure and meaning of helping out at work and in relationships without feeling you shouldn't feel happy about your small efforts?

MAKING A DIFFERENCE AS AN ALTERNATIVE TO THE "BLAME GAME"

Making a difference also provides a pathway for getting results without having to prove we are right and others are wrong. It is a concept that embraces collaboration rather than competition. It is the journey and the destination that provide benefits to self and others, as well as to organizations. The more we notice opportunities to make a difference and push ourselves to rise to the occasion, the better we will feel about ourselves as well as life in general. The funny thing is, these opportunities are all around us. Are you ready to expand your awareness and identify these opportunities and to consciously use the strengths of your personality to make a difference?

2

How Do *You* Make a Difference?

You're the only one who can make the difference.
Whatever your dream is, go for it.
—EARVIN "MAGIC" JOHNSON

Your success at making a difference is a function of three things:

- Your abilities
- Your motivation
- The opportunities that exist in your life

For example, at work your performance is tied to some extent to the abilities you possess to do your job. Your knowledge and skills are what make you capable of doing your work. However, if you are not motivated to apply your abilities, you won't be performing at your best and you won't be making a difference. If you are not clear whether you should be involved in a given task or to what extent the quality and quantity of your efforts are needed, you are less likely to make the most of your abilities. Expectations are an important part of motivation. Furthermore, if your fulfillment of expectations (assuming you fulfill them) is not reinforced, you won't be motivated for long. Finally, though you may have the ability and motivation to do a task, if you are not given the opportunity to perform, you won't have the chance to make a difference. Any athlete who has been relegated to the bench can tell you that. Making a difference is truly a matter of the interaction between your abilities, motivations, and opportunities.

In this chapter we explore how you have made a difference at work and in personal relationships—both inside and outside work—and why your efforts are important to you. This exploration will lead us to how you can purposely use your natural personality preferences to increase your efforts to make a difference. You will be asked to examine your natural abilities, your motivations, and the opportunities that exist at work and in your relationships.

There are so many ways to make a difference. Just to get you started, begin to think about times when you might have helped others by:

- Developing a plan
- Negotiating a settlement
- Catching a mistake before it happened
- Solving a problem
- Reducing the stress in a situation
- Being a role model
- Providing some feedback
- Encouraging others by showing that you care
- Generating enthusiasm
- Communicating information effectively
- Resolving a conflict
- Motivating others
- Influencing a decision
- Providing an ethical standard

- Developing trust
- Showing respect
- Establishing credibility
- Team building
- Helping others feel valued
- Improving the image of a team or company
- Dealing with different personalities
- Remaining healthy in a dysfunctional organization
- Providing leadership
- Developing leadership in others
- Instituting a change
- Caring for others

MAKING A DIFFERENCE AT WORK

Let's begin by looking at how you can make a difference at work. It is in virtually every organization's self-interest to recognize and encourage its employees as they seek the satisfaction of making a difference. Recognition doesn't cost the company money; it enhances morale and leads to greater effectiveness. Even if your employer does not emphasize making a difference, there are still hundreds of ways you can do it if you are willing to take the initiative. When I asked study participants about times when they had made a difference at work, I heard many themes repeated in their stories, such as simplifying things, being positive, rescuing people, developing systems, reducing stress, and so on. Here's one person's story.

> While working at a tuxedo rental store, I often helped
> reduce stress in a typically stressful situation for brides and
> grooms before their wedding day. One wedding party soon
> had to leave to travel for the wedding. Some of the guys

came in a day late for their fittings, and some of the sizes needed to be changed. We didn't keep the tuxedos at the stores—everything was kept at a warehouse nearby. Even though the problem really wasn't our fault, I told the guys I would fix everything. I took down their address, drove to the warehouse, and delivered the replacements to their house so they could leave for the wedding on time.

Use exercise 1 to help you identify some of the ways you have made a difference in job tasks or with people at work. In exercises 14 and 15 in chapter 8 you will be asked to review these events as you are coached to make even more of a difference in your current work situation.

EXERCISE 1

Times When You Made a Difference at Work

In the space below or on a separate sheet of paper write down several examples of times when you have made a difference at work. Don't forget to include the ordinary times—don't discount those experiences. Provide as many details as possible and be specific.

_____

_____

_____

_____

_____

_____

_____

_____

_____

MAKING A DIFFERENCE
IN RELATIONSHIPS

Most people will not feel sufficiently fulfilled by making a difference only at work. Aristotle said, "Without friendship, no happiness is possible." Human beings are social animals and have a fundamental need to love and be loved. Making a difference in relationships with friends, lovers, family, neighbors, coworkers, and others is a key way we show we care and at the same time also get our needs met. We don't necessarily do this to change others. We give of ourselves and make a difference in many ways. When I asked the subjects of my research studies how they had made a difference in relationships, I heard many themes repeated in their stories, such as being dependable, smoothing over conflicts, encouraging risk taking, and helping others increase their competence. Here's another story.

> *I have made a difference with my friend Matt by constantly encouraging him to go back to school. I kept telling him that he is a smart guy and he can handle college easily. He recently decided to enroll at the community college for the winter semester and work on more general education credits before coming back to the university. I like to think that maybe my encouragement and positive remarks might have made a difference.*

Use exercise 2 to help you identify some of the ways you have made a difference in relationships. In exercises 14 and 15 you will be asked to review these events as you are coached to make even more of a difference in your current relationships.

EXERCISE 2

Times When You Made a Difference in Relationships

In the space below or on a separate sheet of paper, write down several examples of times when you have made a difference in your relationships with family members, spouses, lovers, friends, neighbors, or even coworkers outside work. Don't forget to include the ordinary times—don't discount those experiences. Provide as many details as possible and be specific.

_____

_____

_____

_____

_____

_____

_____

_____

_____

_____

_____

_____

_____

WHY IS MAKING A DIFFERENCE IMPORTANT TO YOU?

We all have had moments when we made a difference. These moments have been good for us and good for others. They include everyday events, not just life-changing events. In exercises 1 and 2 you described some times when you made a difference. In exercise 3 you'll be examining the feelings those efforts generated and why making a difference may be an important source of motivation for you.

EXERCISE 3

The Impact of Making a Difference

Review the events you listed in exercises 1 and 2 where you made a difference at work or in relationships. Pick one or more of those events to examine more closely in the space provided below. How did you feel before, during, and after your effort? How did others feel? In particular, why was what you did meaningful to you? Why was it meaningful to the others involved?

_____

_____

_____

_____

_____

_____

_____

Why was what you did pleasurable for you? Why was it pleasurable for the others involved?

_____

_____

_____

_____

_____

_____

continues

Exercise 3 cont'd

How did your making a difference keep you engaged and involved?
What kept you focused?

_____

_____

_____

_____

_____

_____

_____

Based on your answers above, why is making a difference important
to you?

_____

_____

_____

_____

_____

_____

_____

_____

DOES MAKING A DIFFERENCE
MEAN THE SAME TO EVERYONE?

As you think about the many ways to make a difference, you probably will notice some common helping behaviors that anyone can use to make a difference at work or in relationships. Certain situations and people would benefit from variations in the application of these themes. In general, many people try to read the situation or person and respond to the need/want identified. For some people this means trying to be something they are not. This book, in accordance with the positive psychology movement, encourages you to seek happiness primarily through the strengths of your natural personality preferences. My research indicates that your personality produces a style that suits you well in your efforts to make a difference. Chapter 3 will help you understand your own personality and its likely strengths. Chapters 4–7 will help you identify the elements of your core personality type and how you can make better use of it by living your life consciously.

3

Who Are You? Putting Your Personality to Use

A person cannot choose wisely for a life unless he dares to listen to himself, his own self, at each moment in life.
—ABRAHAM MASLOW

Who are you when you are just being yourself? Here are some thoughts on the subject from some of the participants in my research studies on making a difference:

- "The best advice I ever gave someone before he went into a crucial job interview was to 'just be yourself.'"

- "I didn't really know what to tell my people about how to handle the rough situation we were facing, but what helped was my boss telling me to just be myself."

- "My best friend knew I really wanted to go out with Gary. Just before going on my first date with him, she told me to just be myself, because if he didn't like who I am, then he wouldn't be the right guy for me anyway. So here it is now, Gary and I have been happily married for fifteen years and have two beautiful kids. On our best days all we really expect from each other is to be ourselves."

THE ANSWER TO "JUST BE YOURSELF"

Have you ever given someone the classic advice to "just be your-self"? Have you ever received that advice? What does "being your-self" mean to you? Exercise 4 might help start clarifying this for you.

EXERCISE 4

Who Are You?

Answer each of the following questions in the space to the right of the letter below it. Later you will use the space to the left of the letter to rank the importance of your response.

Question A: Pick one word or, at most, a short phrase to answer the question "Who are you?"

_____ A. _____

Question B: Who are you? Answer this question again without using the same word or phrase you used for question A.

_____ B. _____

Questions C–Z: Continue answering the question "Who are you?" In each case use a different word or phrase but make sure every answer really captures an essence of who you are. Stretch your think-ing about yourself and try to complete the entire list. As above, write your answers to the right of the letter.

_____ C. _____

_____ D. _____

_____ E. _____

_____ F. _____

_____ G. _____

_____ H. _____

_____ I. _____

continues

Exercise 4 cont'd

_____ J. _____

_____ K. _____

_____ L. _____

_____ M. _____

_____ N. _____

_____ O. _____

_____ P. _____

_____ Q. _____

_____ R. _____

_____ S. _____

_____ T. _____

_____ U. _____

_____ V. _____

_____ W. _____

_____ X. _____

_____ Y. _____

_____ Z. _____

Now go back and rank your responses, from 1 up to 26 (at least your top ten), putting a "1" to the left of the answer that is the most important element describing the core of who you really are. Put a "2" to the left of the answer that is the next most important element describing the core of who you really are. And so on.

Now let's analyze the words and phrases you chose in exercise 4 and your answer rankings. The answer you ranked #1 you see as most central to the core of who you really are. The remaining items are important elements of the "real" you, but they represent successively more superficial features of your identity as they decline in rank.

FINDING THE "WHOS" BEHIND YOUR "WHATS"

In their work on diversity, Lee Gardenswartz and Anita Rowe (1994) posit that each individual has four dimensions of identity, ranging from the most superficial to the most core:

- The organizational dimension, which includes type of work, department, seniority, union affiliation, etc.

- The external dimension, which includes personal habits, recreational activities, religion, appearance, etc.

- The internal dimension, which includes age, race, ethnicity, physical ability, gender, etc.

- Personality, which includes all aspects and tendencies that may be classified as personal style

In responding to the question "Who are you?" we often respond with an answer from one of Gardenswartz and Rowe's more superficial dimensions. That is, we often respond by saying what we are rather than delving into who we are. Review your answers in exercise 4. Did you sometimes answer the question by listing physical characteristics of what you are, or by identifying yourself with a role you fulfill in life? If so, now try to substitute a word or phrase that captures the "who" behind the "what" for any items where you answered with a description of a superficial aspect of your identity.

For example, if you described yourself as an industrial engineer or a union leader or an executive or a health care provider, what might be behind these organizational roles? Could the "who" behind the "what" of an answer such as "industrial engineer" be a systematic problem solver? Perhaps your answer came from the external dimension and you identified yourself as a midwesterner or a Catholic. If so, what does it tell us about you? Could the "who" behind the "what"—a midwesterner—indicate that you look at life realistically? Or perhaps your answer came from the internal dimension, for example, "I am a man" or "I am a Baby Boomer" or "I am a Polish American." If you listed your ethnic identification, could that mean that a core element of who you are is being a proud and loyal person?

In order to be yourself you have to know yourself. Push yourself to identify the elements of your "who" that underlie the physical qualities as well as personal and occupational roles you play in life. What did exercise 4 teach you about the essence of who you really are? Do these words help you understand how you would behave if someone suggested that you ought to just be yourself? In what way? "Just be yourself" is easy to say but more difficult to put into practice. Each person is a mix of characteristics at several levels. To make a difference more naturally, you will be asked to discover more about your core level—your personality.

DESCRIBING YOUR PERSONALITY TYPE

The next step toward being able to use the strengths of your natural self is to learn how to describe yourself in a more systematic way. Swiss psychologist Carl Jung (1971) developed a framework for understanding personality types in the 1920s, and Isabel Briggs Myers and her mother, Katharine Cook Briggs, later helped refine that framework and developed the *Myers-Briggs Type Indicator*® (MBTI®) instrument. The framework is based on the following assumptions:

- An individual's personality type is determined by his or her preferences in four pairs of opposites, known as preference pairs.
- Neither side of a preference pair is better than the other; in fact, they complement each other.
- People have a natural or more accessible preference for one side of a preference pair over the other, but we all use both to some degree. Just as you may be naturally right-handed,

you can use your left hand when needed—it just won't
seem as natural or comfortable for you.

• The key to a well-developed personality is capitalizing on
your preferences while accepting—even celebrating—
others who show opposite preferences, instead of trying to
be all things to all people or insisting that everyone share
your preferences.

The eight preferences are highlighted in table 1.

Both sides of each preference pair contribute to situations at
work and in relationships. Although personality type is more a
matter of natural tendencies—not of abilities or even specific
behavior—you will be better equipped to make a difference if you
capitalize on the strengths of your natural tendencies. Knowing
your natural tendencies gives you an edge in planning how to
make a difference.

The first preference pair of the Jung/Myers-Briggs® framework, Extraversion–Introversion (E–I), focuses on where you
direct as well as receive energy. People with a preference for Extraversion (E) are more externally oriented, directing their energy
toward and receiving energy from the external world of people
and things. People with a preference for Introversion (I) are more
internally oriented, directing their energy toward and receiving
energy from the internal world of ideas and experiences.

The second preference pair, Sensing–Intuition, describes how
you naturally take in information about what is going on in the
world around you. People with a preference for Sensing (S) tend
to rely on their five senses to focus on the facts, details, and realities
of their present situation. People with a preference for Intuition
(N) tend to look at the world and immediately see possibilities and
the connections between facts and details and what implications
these may have for the future.

The third preference pair, Thinking–Feeling (T–F), looks at
how you tend to make decisions. Those with a preference for
Thinking (T) tend to rely on logic. They prefer to view the world

TABLE 1 The Eight Preferences of the MBTI® Instrument

People with a preference for:	People with a preference for:
E EXTRAVERSION Tend to direct energy toward and receive energy from the external world of people, activities, and things	**I** INTROVERSION Tend to direct energy toward and receive energy from the internal world of ideas and experiences
S SENSING Tend to first perceive immediate, tangible facts through the five senses	**N** INTUITION Tend to first perceive possibilities, patterns, and relationships through insight
T THINKING Tend to make decisions based on logical analysis with a focus on objectivity and detachment	**F** FEELING Tend to make decisions based on personal or social values with a focus on understanding and harmony
J JUDGING Tend to live in a decisive, orderly, planned way and strive for closure in the external world	**P** PERCEIVING Tend to live in a flexible, spontaneous way and strive to stay open to new information in the external world

Source: Adapted from Isabel Briggs Myers, Mary McCaulley, Naomi L. Quenk, and Allen H. Hammer, *MBTI® Manual,* 3rd ed. (Mountain View, CA: CPP, Inc., 2003), 6. Copyright 1998, 2003 by Peter B. Myers and Katharine D. Myers. Used with permission.

objectively and naturally apply the principles of cause and effect to make their decisions. Those with a preference for Feeling (F) tend to be clear about their values and beliefs and want to make decisions consistent with those values and beliefs. They tend to be naturally agreeable unless their values are threatened.

Myers and Briggs added a fourth crucial preference pair, Judging–Perceiving (J–P), which describes how you tend to deal with the outside world. People with a preference for Judging (J) tend to make plans and seek closure, while people with a preference for Perceiving (P) tend to want to be more flexible and spontaneous and to keep their options open.

Altogether, the four preference pairs, comprising eight preferences, create sixteen possible four-letter type combinations, as outlined in table 2, on pages 28–29. For more detailed information on the sixteen types, the interested reader might want to start with the booklet *Introduction to Type*® by Isabel Briggs Myers (1998).

DISCOVERING YOUR
PERSONALITY TYPE

Now it's time to take your wonderfully complex personality and consolidate it into one of those sixteen four-letter types.

Determining your four-letter type can help you understand so much about who you are. Exercise 5, on pages 30–34, is intended to provide a quick and easy way to help you do this, whether or not you have taken the MBTI assessment previously. Keep in mind that it is no substitute for taking the actual assessment and receiving a professional interpretation. You can contact the Association for Psychological Type International, at www.aptinternational.org, to identify a certified professional in your area. Alternatively, you can contact CPP, Inc., at www.cpp.com, to access the online program MBTI®Complete, which enables you to take the full assessment at your own pace, determine your preferences, verify your type, and receive a detailed feedback report explaining your results. Davies-Black Publishing is offering readers a 20 percent discount to take this assessment. Log on to www.mbticomplete.com using the following password: MAD08.

Regardless of which option you choose to identify your type, you will need to verify your "best-fit" type. The certified professional who administers the MBTI assessment to you will have exercises to help you do this. MBTI®Complete includes similar exercises. The four charts in appendix A in this book can also help you verify your best-fit type.

THE FOUR CORE PERSONALITY TYPES

The two middle preference pairs—Sensing–Intuition (S–N) and Thinking–Feeling (T–F)—account for the dominant and auxiliary functions of your personality: the core part of who you are and the secondary part that supports that function. These two middle letters of your four-letter type together form what I call your *core personality type*—the focus of this book. The four possible combinations of middle letters are ST, SF, NF, and NT. Learning about your core personality type can help you use your strengths to make a difference. The four core personality types will be referred to throughout the rest of the book as:

- **Stabilizers (STs)**—tend to be matter-of-fact and have and appreciate common sense. At their core, they generally value getting to the facts and the logic of the matter.
- **Harmonizers (SFs)**—tend to be very sociable and friendly. At their core, they generally value individual relationships.
- **Catalysts (NFs)**—tend to be good communicators who believe in championing causes for the good of others. At their core, they generally want to motivate people to do what's right.
- **Visionaries (NTs)**—tend to be big-picture oriented. At their core, they generally want to develop a blueprint or system for the future.

The Four Core Personality Types at Work

Traditionally, people at work have been expected to behave in accordance with their job title. However, over the past thirty years there has been an increased emphasis on making greater use of

TABLE 2 Characteristics Frequently Associated with the Sixteen Types

ISTJ

Quiet, serious, earn success by thoroughness and dependability. Practical, matter-of-fact, realistic, and responsible. Decide logically what should be done and work toward it steadily, regardless of distractions. Take pleasure in making everything orderly and organized—their work, their home, their life. Value traditions and loyalty.

ISFJ

Quiet, friendly, responsible, and conscientious. Committed and steady in meeting their obligations. Thorough, painstaking, and accurate. Loyal, considerate, notice and remember specifics about people who are important to them, concerned with how others feel. Strive to create an orderly and harmonious environment at work and at home.

ISTP

Tolerant and flexible, quiet observers until a problem appears, then act quickly to find workable solutions. Analyze what makes things work and readily get through large amounts of data to isolate the core of practical problems. Interested in cause and effect, organize facts using logical principles, value efficiency.

ISFP

Quiet, friendly, sensitive, and kind. Enjoy the present moment, what's going on around them. Like to have their own space and to work within their own time frame. Loyal and committed to their values and to people who are important to them. Dislike disagreements and conflicts, do not force their opinions or values on others.

ESTP

Flexible and tolerant, they take a pragmatic approach focused on immediate results. Theories and conceptual explanations bore them—they want to act energetically to solve the problem. Focus on the here and now, spontaneous, enjoy each moment that they can be active with others. Enjoy material comforts and style. Learn best through doing.

ESFP

Outgoing, friendly, and accepting. Exuberant lovers of life, people, and material comforts. Enjoy working with others to make things happen. Bring common sense and a realistic approach to their work, and make work fun. Flexible and spontaneous, adapt readily to new people and environments. Learn best by trying a new skill with other people.

ESTJ

Practical, realistic, matter-of-fact. Decisive, quickly move to implement decisions. Organize projects and people to get things done, focus on getting results in the most efficient way. Take care of routine details. Have clear set of logical standards, systematically follow them and want others to do so. Forceful in implementing their plans.

ESFJ

Warmhearted, conscientious, cooperative. Want harmony and work in determination to establish it. Like to work with others to finish tasks on time and accurately. Loyal, follow through in small matters. Notice what others need in their day-to-day lives and try to provide it. Want to be appreciated for who they are and for what they contribute.

INFJ

Seek meaning and connection in ideas, relationships, and material possessions. Want to understand what motivates people and are insightful about others. Conscientious and committed to their firm values. Develop a clear vision about how best to serve the common good. Organized and decisive in implementing their vision.

INTJ

Have original minds and great drive for implementing their ideas and achieving their goals. Quickly see patterns in external events and develop long-range explanatory perspectives. When committed, organize a job and carry it through. Skeptical and independent, have high standards of competence and performance—for themselves and others.

INFP

Idealistic, loyal to their values and to people who are important to them. Want an external life that is congruent with their values. Curious, quick to see possibilities, can be catalysts for implementing ideas. Seek to understand people and to help them fulfill their potential. Adaptable, flexible, and accepting unless a value is threatened.

INTP

Seek to develop logical explanations for everything that interests them. Theoretical and abstract, interested more in ideas than in social interaction. Quiet, contained, flexible, and adaptable. Have unusual ability to focus in depth to solve problems in their area of interest. Skeptical, sometimes critical, always analytical.

ENFP

Warmly enthusiastic and imaginative. See life as full of possibilities. Make connections between events and information very quickly, and confidently proceed based on the patterns they see. Want a lot of affirmation from others, and readily give appreciation and support. Spontaneous and flexible, often rely on their ability to improvise and their verbal fluency.

ENTP

Quick, ingenious, stimulating, alert, and outspoken. Resourceful in solving new and challenging problems. Adept at generating conceptual possibilities and then analyzing them strategically. Good at reading other people. Bored by routine, will seldom do the same thing the same way, apt to turn to one new interest after another.

ENFJ

Warm, empathetic, responsive, and responsible. Highly attuned to others' emotions, needs, and motivations. Find potential in everyone, want to help others fulfill their potential. May act as catalysts for individual and group growth. Loyal, responsive to praise and criticism. Sociable, facilitate others in a group, and provide inspiring leadership.

ENTJ

Frank, decisive, assume leadership readily. Quickly see illogical and inefficient procedures and policies, develop and implement systems to solve problems. Enjoy long-term planning and goal setting. Usually well informed, well read, enjoy expanding knowledge and sharing it. Forceful in presenting their ideas.

Source: Adapted from Isabel B. Myers, with Linda K. Kirby and Katharine D. Myers, *Introduction to Type,* 6th ed. (Mountain View, CA: CPP, Inc., 1998), 13. Copyright 1998 by Peter B. Myers and Katharine D. Myers. Used with permission.

A Quick Estimate of Your Personality Type Preferences

For each preference pair below, circle the preference option in each set of questions that best describes you across different situations.

Extraversion (E) or Introversion (I)

1. Is your attention directed more externally, toward the world of people and things? (E)
Or, is it directed more internally, toward the internal world of ideas and experiences? (I)

2. Are you more likely to take action and then (maybe) reflect on it later? (E)
Or, are you more likely to think about it a lot and then (maybe) take action? (I)

3. Do you often find yourself thinking out loud? (E)
Or, do you find yourself thinking a lot before saying things aloud? (I)

4. Do you find yourself gaining a lot of energy by interacting with people? (E)
Or, do you find your energy being drained by interacting with people and thus need some downtime to recharge your batteries? (I)

5. Do you tend to have very broad interests? (E)
Or, do you have few but in-depth interests? (I)

6. Do you think of yourself as having many relationships, meeting and talking to people easily? (E)
Or, do you make a big distinction between friends and acquaintances and find small talk difficult? (I)?

7. Do you tend to notice much of what is going on around you and not really mind interruptions? (E)
Or, do you hate to be interrupted and feel more comfortable with silence than do most people? (I)

8. Are you quite willing to share what you think or feel? (E)
Or, do you tend to wait to be asked about what you think or feel before you share? (I)

continues

Exercise 5 cont'd

9. Do you learn best through doing and discussing? (E)
Or, do you learn best through reflection and "mental practice"? (I)

Number of times you circled the E option = _____ 3 4 _____
Number of times you circled the I option = _____ 4 5 _____

Sensing (S) or Intuition (N)

1. Are you more interested in the facts of a situation? (S)
Or, are you more interested in the possibilities of a situation? (N)

2. Do you tend to pay attention to the details? (S)
Or, do you tend to notice the patterns? (N)

3. Are you more patient with routines? (S)
Or, are you more patient with complexity? (N)

4. Do people tend to describe you as sensible, practical, pragmatic, and down-to-earth? (S)
Or, do people tend to describe you as imaginative, innovative, creative, and idealistic? (N)

5. Are you typically more oriented toward the present and thus attend to what is happening here and now? (S)
Or, are you typically more future oriented and keep thinking about what could be? (N)

6. Do you mistrust your intuition and try to prove things to yourself and others in a careful, step-by-step fashion? (S)
Or, once your gut tells you the answer, are you willing to ignore some facts and go with a hunch? (N)

7. Do you consider yourself to have a lot of common sense and prefer people who also have a lot of common sense? (S)
Or, do you consider yourself to be creative and prefer people who are also creative? (N)

8. Do you find yourself responding to what people say literally? (S)
Or, do you find yourself reading between the lines and trying to figure out what they mean? (N)

continues

Exercise 5 cont'd

9. Do you value practical, hands-on experience as the best way
to learn? (S)
Or, do you value learning that comes from inspiration and
conceptualization? (N)

> Number of times you circled the S option = ___5___
> Number of times you circled the N option = ___4___

Thinking (T) or Feeling (F)

1. Do you prefer to use the principles of cause-and-effect logic to
come to a conclusion? (T)
Or, do you prefer to apply your values and beliefs to come to
a conclusion? (F)

2. Do you prefer things to be objective and thus either true or false? (T)
Or, do you prefer to decide first whether you agree or disagree
with something and thus have a more subjective orientation? (F)

3. Do you tend to come across as impersonal even when you really
don't mean to be? (T)
Or, do you tend to come across as naturally friendly unless your
values are threatened? (F)

4. Do you tend to be analytical, skeptical, and questioning? (T)
Or, are you typically trusting and maybe overly accepting? (F)

5. Are you likely to choose truth over tact and thus state things
bluntly? (T)
Or, are you likely to choose tact over truth and thus smooth over
negative comments? (F)

6. Do you appreciate a good argument because it allows an opportunity for both sides of an issue to be brought out into the open? (T)
Or, do you tend to dislike, even fear, conflict and try to keep things
harmonious? (F)

7. Is your idea of justice to treat everyone the same? (T)
Or, is your idea of justice to treat people according to their
needs? (F)

continues

Exercise 5 cont'd

8. Do you tend to take good work for granted, your own as well as that of others? (T)
Or, do you express appreciation readily and probably want it too? (F)

9. Are you more concerned with being reasonable and focusing on the task? (T)
Or, are you more concerned with being compassionate and focusing on relationships? (F)

Number of times you circled the T option = ___7 6___
Number of times you circled the F option = ___2 3___

Judging (J) or Perceiving (P)

1. Do you tend to push for closure in situations? (J)
Or, do you tend to push for understanding in situations? (P)

2. Do you get your greatest pleasure from finishing things? (J)
Or, do you get your greatest pleasure from starting things? (P)

3. Do you tend to be more decisive and purposeful? (J)
Or, do you tend to be more flexible? (P)

4. Do you prefer to make the decision? (J)
Or, do you prefer to generate the options? (P)

5. Do you prefer a planned and orderly approach to things? (J)
Or, do you prefer a more casual and spontaneous approach to things? (P)

6. Do you like to keep to schedules and to-do lists and organize your time accordingly? (J)
Or, do you like to respond to things as they arise? (P)

7. Do you want to have things decided well in advance and then stick to those decisions? (J)
Or, do you want to keep your options open (P)?

continues

Exercise 5 cont'd

8. Do you take deadlines seriously and try to get things done early in order to avoid last-minute stress? (J)
Or, do you use deadlines as a stimulus to get started and feel energized by last-minute pressures? (P)

9. Do you cut off information and make decisions quickly? (J)
Or, do you seek out lots of information, maybe even more than you need? (P)

Number of times you circled the J option = ___7___ 6 _____
Number of times you circled the P option = ___2___ 3 _____

Determine Your Personality Type

Taking your top-scoring preference options from each preference pair listed above, enter them below to form your four-letter type. (For example, if you circled E six times and I three times, you would enter E on the "E or I" line below.)

I̶E̶   S̲   T̲   J̲
E or I   S or N   T or F   J or P

Remember to use the four charts in appendix A to help verify your best-fit type.

people's full potential. The use of terms such as *employee involvement, job enrichment,* and *self-managing teams* has increased steadily in American, Japanese, and European workplaces. Jobs have become less narrowly defined, and in many companies people have been asked to take on a broader range of responsibilities. The impact of these strategies can be positive on both organizational performance and employee morale. Ninety percent of Fortune 1000 companies now provide their employees with the opportunity to get involved and make a difference. While some companies still seem to focus more on catching workers making a mistake than on employees making a difference, research by David Cooperrider and Suresh Srivastra (1987) has shown that focusing on what has worked can add more value to organizational change efforts than can analyzing past errors. Furthermore, research by James O'Toole and Edward Lawler (2006) and many others suggests that making a difference is key to workers' having a satisfying and productive work life, and provides employees with pleasure, a sense of meaning, and an opportunity to feel engaged—the three dimensions advocated by Martin Seligman (2004) in his seminal work on positive psychology, *Authentic Happiness.*

Appendix B, "Your Core Personality Type at Work," presents another exercise for estimating your type preferences. It focuses solely on the four core personality types and how your personality manifests itself at work. If you are specifically trying to discover additional ways to make a difference at work, turn to appendix B now and complete that exercise. You may also want to turn to appendix A to help confirm your best-fit type.

Living Your Life Consciously

All humans are creatures of habit to some extent. Habits help us find comfortable ways of handling the routine aspects of life at work and elsewhere. However, when our habits restrict our ability to make choices to improve our life and that of others, we fail to increase our opportunities to make a difference. When habits are used merely to pass time, we may be wasting a precious commodity. After all, life is short! How often do you find yourself "killing" time? Matthieu Ricard (2006) points out that we could be *enlivening* time instead of killing it. Are you ready to choose to use time more consciously to make a difference? No one can control everything, but we all can become aware of our approach to life and take responsibility for the decisions we make. This is the essence of several well-known approaches to coaching leaders in work situations, such as *Go Put Your Strengths to Work* by Marcus Buckingham (2007), *Enhancing Leadership Effectiveness Through Psychological Type* by Roger Pearman (1999), and *Introduction to Type® and*

Coaching by Sandra Hirsh and Jane Kise (2000); and to approaches to helping people with personal problems, such as *Choice Theory* by William Glasser (1998) and *A Guide to Rational Living* by Albert Ellis and Robert Harper (1974).

What if you chose to go beyond taking yourself, as well as your situations, for granted and decided to plan how you are going to make a difference for others this week? And then what if you did this again next week, and the week after that, and so on until it became a habit? According to Aristotle, "We first make our habits and then our habits make us." You have gifts to offer the world based on the core elements of who you are. Isabel Briggs Myers identified the different gifts offered by each MBTI personality type in her book *Gifts Differing* (1980). What is your personal sense of responsibility for providing the people in your world with your gifts? What is your personal sense of responsibility for developing your gifts further? Chapters 4–7 provide a number of opportunities to identify ways to use your personality more.

Living your life consciously by being yourself is the key strategy for making a difference. In fact, the more you experience life in a manner that is not in tune with who you are, the more you will feel *beside* yourself. Naomi Quenk's marvelous book *Beside Ourselves* (1993; revised as *Was That Really Me?*, 2002) points out that under stressful conditions we act out by using the least developed and least conscious elements of our personality, leading us into many of the difficulties we experience at work and in our relationships.

Certainly, we can't always make things happen just because we want them to happen or prevent all unpleasant events just by living our life consciously. In fact, research on what is known as "fundamental attribution error" (see Kelley 1975 and Weiner 1985) suggests that our behaviors are more a function of our reactions to situations than a reflection of our personal characteristics. Personality type, especially as identified by the MBTI framework, captures only a person's natural preferences—and these may or may not be expressed behaviorally. What is it going to take to get you to live your life consciously at least on those occasions when using your preferences might enable you to make a difference? Are you ready to go beyond your habits, to go beyond merely reacting to situations, to go beyond merely understanding the insights of your personality type results and actually use the strengths of your personality? It all starts with you. What are you doing that is meaningful, that makes you and others happier and better off? Carl Jung (1955) pointed out that "the least of things with meaning is worth more in life than the greatest things without it."

PUTTING YOUR PERSONALITY TO USE

To what extent are you using the natural strengths associated with your personality in any given week? Buckingham (2000) reports research results showing that only 20 percent of people feel they can put their strengths to work every day and only 17 percent of people feel they can use their strengths most of the time at work. What if you decided to capitalize on the strengths of who you really are just 10 percent more than you ordinarily do in any given week? You don't need to spend most of your waking time consciously using the strengths of your personality; just try to use them more often than you are currently using them.

You already acknowledged in exercises 1 and 2 that you have made a difference at work and in your relationships. Now it's time for you to use what you have learned about who you are and increase your pool of ideas about how to make a difference. Each of the following four chapters examines how individuals of one of the core personality types—Stabilizer, Harmonizer, Catalyst, or Visionary—have used their personality preferences to make a difference. You may want to read all four chapters, but be sure to read carefully the one specifically written about you.

Making a Difference
with *Your* Personality

Each of the following four chapters focuses on one of the four core personality types: Stabilizers (STs), Harmonizers (SFs), Catalysts (NFs), and Visionaries (NTs). You might want to go directly to the chapter on what you believe to be your core personality type to help confirm your self-assessment. Or, you might want to go to the chapter on the core personality type of individuals you are coaching or helping in some manner. This may give you insights into how to better reach out to these people and help them make a difference in their work and relationships. Or, since to some degree we all share some characteristics of each core type, you might want to read all four chapters to discover new and different ways in which you can make a difference.

The beginning of each chapter offers a few key things to know about that particular core personality type through a "scouting report" on people who report these preferences. That's followed by a more detailed description of the tendencies of these people. The largest section of each chapter—a series of true stories provided by study participants with the core personality type and how they went about making a difference at work and in their relationships—is organized by the key themes (ten at work and ten in relationships) identified for that type.

It is recommended that you highlight ideas you gain from the descriptions of the tendencies of a core type and especially the strategies and tactics people used to make a difference. You will be asked to develop plans to increase the frequency with which you make a difference at your work and in your relationships in chapter 8. Perhaps you can learn vicariously from the experiences reported in the stories.

People of all core personality types have much to offer at work and in relationships. You can especially make a difference in ways that capitalize on the strengths of your natural preferences. When you are being your true self, those preferences are likely to shine. However, no individual is (or should be) true to his or her preferences in all situations.

A FEW NOTES ON THE RESEARCH STUDIES

From 2003 to 2008 I conducted a series of research studies that resulted in three presentations at the biannual meetings of the Association for Psychological Type International. This book contains the accumulated highlights across these studies.

For the studies over five hundred participants were recruited from a variety of sources. Some were attendees of APT chapter presentations; some were members of organizations for which I served as an OD consultant; others included graduate students or undergraduate seniors enrolled in my course on organizational change. They all completed a lengthy questionnaire with a demographic section in which they were asked to reveal their MBTI best-fit type. The questionnaire also included open-ended questions about times when they had made a difference at work, in a relationship, or in their community. Most participants also completed a section of fixed-format questions asking them to rate the degree to which they utilized various strategies and tactics to make a difference.

A team of graduate students then read all of the more than fifteen hundred stories generated. They were asked to identify the themes in the stories "blind to type"—that is, they had only the written portion of the questionnaire containing the stories, without access to the MBTI type of the storyteller. A series of discussions was facilitated to obtain rater agreement on the themes of the stories. Then the type of the storyteller was reattached to the questionnaire, and those themes that were disproportionately reported for a given type were identified. This—along with a subsequent analysis of the fixed-format questions—is how the themes reported in chapters 4–7 were originally produced. Some of the themes were consolidated to enhance the readability of this book.

It is my hope that this book thus combines the best of both worlds: the processes of systematic research methodologies and practical guidance for use of the results. It should help readers move beyond insight and understanding to actually putting to use their core personality type to make a difference!

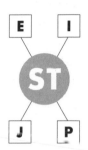

How "Stabilizers" (STs) Can Make a Difference

People with preferences for Sensing (S) and Thinking (T) tend to be very matter-of-fact and have and appreciate common sense. We will refer to these ST types as "Stabilizers." If you have determined by looking at the middle preferences of your four-letter MBTI type that you are a Stabilizer (that is, an ST), this chapter is especially for you. You may also want to read this chapter to learn more about others who have this core personality type.

We'll start with a "scouting report" on people with this core personality type and then move to a more detailed description of these and other tendencies reported in the research studies.

Scouting Report on Stabilizers

Stabilizers tend to . . .

- Be practical and matter-of-fact
- Have and appreciate common sense
- Be competitive and efficient
- Solve problems step by step, creating incremental progress
- Prefer specific and detailed structures, roles, procedures, and formats

continues

Stabilizers cont'd

- Want to be shown that something is broken before they want to fix it
- Be concerned about worst-case scenarios
- Use tried-and-true, proven methods
- Focus on the here and now in a rational way
- Pay attention to details and logic

Overall, Stabilizers tend to make a difference . . .

- **At work** by breaking down complex issues into a series of steps and tasks that can help bring practical results
- **In relationships** by providing a matter-of-fact approach that can help people deal with emotional issues in a dependable, calm, and less stressful manner

A MORE DETAILED LOOK AT STABILIZERS

First of all, be sure to keep in mind that the descriptions of Stabilizers that follow reflect general tendencies only. They are not true for all people with preferences for Sensing and Thinking. Furthermore, people with any of the other three core personality types could be found to exhibit the characteristics provided in the descriptions because situations—as well as personality preferences—drive behavior. Nevertheless, *in general,* these descriptions will help in your understanding of the Stabilizer core personality type.

Stabilizers tend to be interested in facts and details and prefer to focus on the task at hand and analyze situations in an objective and logical manner. They are typically practical and matter-of-fact. They often use their area of expertise to make a difference in all kinds of ways. Their strengths can lead them into administrative positions, where they can provide a regular, structured approach to doing business. They favor people and organizations that operate efficiently. They may enjoy looking at tabular reports of information to understand a situation and come to conclusions in a rational manner that does not require long meetings with lots of people.

Stabilizers often learn best in a well-defined and structured setting. Their main interest is in facts that can be collected and verified through the senses (e.g., seeing, hearing, touching, etc.). They trust the logical, linear process of cause-and-effect analysis in coming to conclusions. They want to solve personal problems in an objective manner and may shy away from most forms of personal counseling for themselves or others. Their efforts to help people often feature a behavior modification approach that produces incremental progress.

Stabilizers provide leadership to organizations by establishing or supporting a detailed, practical, steady but patient strategy. They want to pursue goals that are realistic, down-to-earth, and economical. They want the facts to be heavily documented and to focus on one step at a time. They may be more interested in micro than macro issues. They want the organizational structure to be very logical with very clear channels for communication, with checks and balances built in to reduce risks. They pay attention to the physical features of the work environment with an eye toward practicality. They prefer job descriptions to be quite detailed and they like (or at least can survive) a bureaucracy perhaps better than any other type. They set up or support clear business procedures and routines. They prefer formats for reports and rely on hard data and experience in decision making.

Stabilizers' leadership style tends to be dependable, realistic, fair, and detail and fact oriented. They want to make plans and then have people follow the plans. They may come across as blunt and decisive and tend to reward compliance while holding people accountable. They tend to hire people who respond well to rules and show common sense. They are good at routines and want meetings and reports to be efficient.

On teams, Stabilizers may gravitate to roles that help the team manage costs, schedules, and statistics. They want the team to use proven methods to increase performance and to solve problems as they arise. They want the team to focus on what is going on now and may not contribute as much to sessions hypothesizing about the future. They also might not be particularly fond of self-aware-ness exercises or brainstorming activities that don't seem to be leading to an immediate practical outcome.

Stabilizers often value stability, dependability, orderliness, practicality, fairness, honesty, objectivity, competitiveness, and security. They can be tough-minded managers who get others to do the job. They like to feel that things are under control. They tend not to like people who like to rock the boat and don't particu-larly like to deal with uncertainties. They may mistakenly treat strategy as an end rather than a means, may overly guard against catastrophe, come across as too impersonal and matter-of-fact, overrely on formulas for decision making, and forget to praise people. They are great at making sure things get measured. They need to be convinced that change is necessary because something is broken. They want to know the specific benefits of applications and may ask a lot of questions.

Stabilizers can contribute to work situations in many wonder-ful ways and they tend to use these same approaches in their per-sonal relationships, too. Perhaps more than any other type, they exhibit the "you can depend on me" attitude without necessarily showing a personal attachment. They help others focus on pres-ent-day realities while nonchalantly fixing problems, even emo-tionally laden ones, and following through on the steps of an implementation plan. Their notion of fairness often helps ensure that everyone is treated equally. These are dependable, practical, logical problem solvers who can help people get through difficult times one step at a time.

HOW STABILIZERS (STs) TEND TO DIFFER

Of course, not all Stabilizers are alike. For example, STs who also have preferences for Extraversion and Judging (ESTJs) tend to generate solutions to problems in a take-charge manner. Plus, they are likely to prefer a detailed and orderly approach that spells out more precisely who is to do what with whom by when, whereas ESTPs often have a tendency to just get some action started and then see where it leads. Introverted STs (ISTs) are often careful compilers working behind the scenes and may generate files of facts that can prove to be useful for planning or measuring progress. Introverted STs with a preference for Perceiving (ISTPs) may generate solutions by offering numerous options to choose from.

STABILIZERS (STs) MAKING A DIFFERENCE AT WORK

Let's look at how Stabilizers, when using the strengths of their natural preferences, can make a difference at work. Each of the following themes represents characteristics expressed by Stabilizer participants from the research studies. Each theme is illustrated by stories written by the participants, with the storyteller's four-letter type provided at the end of each story.

Theme 1: Simplifying Things

Stabilizers can make a difference by using their natural preferences to produce order, schedules, and short-term plans and goals. STJs especially often attempt to clarify expectations, make things easier, and standardize procedures. Many a workplace has benefited from their ability to identify the steps needed to implement an activity or other action.

> *I work at an engineering firm that provides trackside support for the Indy car races. The engineers felt stressed. I provide all the arrangements and times for work at the tracks in order for them to be on time and to know the most recent updated travel arrangements. They would often lose itineraries, and I developed a simple solution to their problem and reduced*

*some of their stress. I laminated a card with all travel require-
ments and track times on it. Engineers were given an annual
pass, which they would hang around their neck.*   **(ESTJ)**

*When I was working for the city's athletic department, we
had a problem scheduling makeup games for Little League
baseball games. We were running out of time to get these
games in, so I came up with a simple but firm plan to tell
my coworkers. My plan was to have all the makeup games
on a certain weekend so that teams and umpires would be
available all day. I then just scheduled the games. If the
team was unable to make it or just didn't show up, they
would have to forfeit.*   **(ESTJ)**

*I had to reorganize a nursery. I moved plants to places
where they were not only easier to care for but also easiest
to sell. It was the most profitable year ever.*   **(ISTP)**

*As an automotive technician I helped the male mechanics
get a better understanding of vehicular symptoms/problems
given by female drivers/customers—that is, I simply inter-
preted "female speak" into "male speak."*   **(ESTJ)**

Theme 2: Getting It Done

Stabilizers are likely to be realistic. STJs especially tend to push for
measurable results such as cost savings, productivity, and profits.
They often want to see tasks and meetings completed efficiently.
They can help teams meet deadlines and save time and money.

*I work for a phone company and was assigned to clean up
invoices for one of their large commercial accounts. I was
brought in to help clean up two thousand invoices, and when
I started, the balance for the year was $800,000. I was suc-
cessful in providing credits and getting payment completed*

in five months. This made a difference at work because this was the first time in the history of this account that the invoices were cleaned up within a year of when the invoice was issued.   **(ESTJ)**

I am a technical trainer. As I was doing training and learning more about the bank, I saw a need for an intranet. Branches were submitting reports twenty-one different ways. Information was mainly flowing on paper. I took it upon myself to build the intranet in my spare time while keeping my other commitments. It has helped everyone in the back save paper costs and helped workflow and made things easier for everyone.   **(ESTJ)**

After three years of lifeguarding, I thought my lifesaving days were over. I had been hired by an excavating company between my freshman and sophomore years of college and was satisfied doing manual labor because of the high pay. Little did I know that within the first week on the job I was going to have to save my own foreman's life! We were finished digging the trenches of an apartment building's basement and had just begun filling them with cement when I heard a loud scream. I turned around from my work just in time to see my foreman Rusty do a face-plant into an eight-foot pool of cement that had just been poured by a cement truck. My lifeguard training instantly kicked in as I rushed over to save my boss. Unlike in a swimming pool, it took all my strength to pull my 250-pound boss out of the cement. Luckily for him, nothing was damaged except his tool belt— and pride.   **(ISTJ)**

Theme 3: Moving One Step at a Time

Stabilizers generally don't mind learning by trial and error. They can get others to try pilot efforts before buying into a system whole-hog. They can also encourage slow but steady progress, making a difference by ensuring that others don't try to do too much too fast.

> *I have been working in HR for the past five years. For the past year, I have been working in an automotive manufacturing plant with four hundred employees from all different backgrounds. I was met with hesitation when I first started there. The HR department had a huge turnover rate. I was doing not just benefits administration but a lot of employee relations. The hourly workforce saw a new face in the department, and I became bait for a disgruntled bunch. I decided to start some routines to show people I am dependable. The workforce is predominantly black, and I was looked upon as another "white girl" in a salaried position. Impressions began to change within a few months, though. Not many salaried people (including the HR staff) go on the plant floor. I began to make my rounds every day on all three shifts just to see how the employees were and answer any questions. The glares began to stop and some employees started asking me how I was doing. Some of the ones who gave me such a difficult time in the beginning are the same ones now asking me not to quit or find a new job.* (ESTJ)

> *I work at an auto parts store as a salesman/counterman. Much of our time is spent looking up and ordering parts. Up until about two years ago, we had placed orders by hand-writing an order slip and calling the order into our warehouse. Of course with computers this process could be done much more efficiently. About two years ago we upgraded our computer system and also got each computer system hooked up to the Internet. Now instead of hand-writing orders and calling them in, we could generate a quote and order the parts electronically. Most of us younger guys thought this was great—we grew up around computers. But*

the guys who have been doing things the old way for years were reluctant to change. I suggested that we could phase the new way in: If you have time, try the new way—it may be slower at first, but once you get the hang of it, it will be that much quicker. If you are busy, call it in and next time try the new way. Once the guys got comfortable with the computers we found that they preferred to order that way because it has so many nice features. The lesson I learned is that change can take time, but it is necessary.   **(ISTJ)**

I am the manager of a computer support group, working to support the research and teaching efforts at the School of Medicine. I manage the staff, providing hands-on support of machines and first-level networking issues. Our department has experienced rapid growth over the past three years— from a staffing level of four to our current level of thirty-seven. I came on board just as the growth was beginning. I've had to learn a lot of what I'm doing now by trial and error, and by what I saw working well in previous jobs, and trying to avoid mistakes I saw happening, also. I think we're doing well—one measure is the increase in calls we get from areas that we're slowly penetrating into, where we're getting buy-in to our change, and the uniformly positive comments and responses we get from our users and the new first-time contacts.   **(ESTJ)**

Theme 4: Catching and Correcting Mistakes

Stabilizers often catch mistakes and prevent problems before they cost a company money or embarrassment. They tend to double-check their work and that of others and often make good inspectors and proofreaders.

I was working with my father and checking out the condos/ commercial property that he built. I found some flaws in the *framework on the stairs and some other imperfections. The biggest role I played was catching some mismatched numbers on a balance sheet. The accountant forgot to report almost $50,000 on the assets side. I noticed this and told my dad. I currently work for a carpet-cleaning firm. I found a flaw in how we cleaned carpeted stairways. I found a better tool to attach the hose to the staircase so it didn't slide down the stairs. It was first done with a back that scuffed the staircase, and customers did not like that. I found that the Velcro that attached the hose links worked very well for it.* **(ESTJ)**

A difference that I made in a work situation was catching an error before it happened. I was working as a grounds crew member at a school district. The weed whippers ran on a combination of gas and oil and must be filled right in order to have fuel for the whippers. On one occasion one of the mechanics that mixed the gas and oil together used too much oil. This would damage the engine. The whipper would have sat for weeks in order to get repaired or it could have been rendered unusable. Either way the expense would have been high. I noticed he had mixed in too much oil and I brought it to his attention. He was grateful, as he would have gotten in trouble. By noting the problem I saved the school hundreds of dollars. **(ESTP)**

I feel that one of the most important contributions I made was catching a mistake in a letter before it was sent. The letter was to be sent to business professionals, faculty, staff, and students. My job was to simply mail the letters. However, I knew that this was a huge project that people would be calling to RSVP or to ask questions in regards to the letter. So I decided to read the letter so I would know exactly how it was worded to better help answer questions that people may have had about the contents of the letter. As I read the letter I noticed a mistake: it had the wrong month of the celebration. I brought it to the attention of the office staff, and they were amazed. All five of them had read the letter and not noticed the mistake. To say the least, they were very thankful to me.   **(ISTJ)**

Theme 5: Just Getting to Work

Stabilizers often prefer to break a task down into steps. They tend to want to get things started and take the initiative—especially the ESTs. They seldom slack off and are usually willing to take on the heavy/dirty work.

There is a lot of downtime at my work, during which employees tend to slack off, even though there are a number of jobs they could be doing. I have noticed that when I take the initiative to clean something, stack a cooler, talk to a customer, many of the other employees will act in a similar way. This is much more effective than simply telling them to do something.   **(ESTJ)**

I worked for Pepsi as a merchandiser. The job was to go to different stores and fill the shelves, build and maintain displays, and keep the back room organized and clean. One day I was stationed at a large supermarket for ten hours. When we ran a sale, they couldn't keep our pop on the shelf. However, this particular day turned out to be slow. I had already filled the shelves and the displays and was finishing in the back room. I noticed that this store had a problem in the bottle return area. They were short-staffed and had returnables all over. I went and helped them for three hours. As a result everything was organized and in the right bin. That night my boss called me and told me I did a hell of a job. Come to find out, Pepsi was having problems getting good spots for their sales. The next day I got to pull Coke out of the center aisle and put Pepsi there. I was rewarded because I took time to help them.   **(ISTP)**

Approximately one year ago, the team leader secretary at work left after thirteen years. I was asked to take her job. However, I refused, due to the fact that I knew I would be leaving the company when I finished school this summer. Over the past year, it has been very difficult filling this position. In the interim, I have taken on many of the team leader tasks that have not been getting done. I was not asked to take on the added responsibility. I just do it because I know it needs to be done. I haven't brought it to anyone's attention that I have taken on more responsibility. This extra effort on my part has helped to make the loss of the team leader secretary an easier burden on the firm.   **(ISTJ)**

Theme 6: Being Dependable

Stabilizers tend to be loyal to their employers. They are reliable, show up for work, and act responsibly. STJs in particular are likely to follow through on specific tasks.

I would always show up on time when I was in a previous child care position. There were five workers and fifty kids. Others would come in late often. On one day I was the only one on time and the kids came in. If I wasn't there, the kids would have been alone.   **(ESTJ)**

When I was a head waitress at a restaurant I had to be a role model for regular servers—clean clothes (uniform), conservative looks, polite, disciplined, always completing assigned tasks. I couldn't let myself be a slacker because forty servers were always watching and learning from my example. If I would do something wrong—not punch out on break to go to the restroom, for example—they would think it was right and do the same thing. Sometimes it's hard to be a role model.   **(ISTJ)**

One of the jobs I have made a difference in was working at a retail store. I started by reorganizing our company's memos, sales, and other papers that needed to be filed. I helped remodel a part of the store to enhance merchandise visibility for our customers. I was a head cashier, but the managers had me working as an assistant manager also. I was always on time with the paperwork and with the store's daily sales figures. I usually came in to work when someone called off. I knew I was an asset to the company. I was doing work for the other employees and managers. I always ended up being the information source, because I knew the company's procedures and how to manage conflict with the customers. When any of my fellow employees were unable to handle a customer complaint, I was the person to deal with their problems. **(ISTJ)**

Theme 7: Establishing Accountability

Stabilizers tend to want to know who is supposed to be doing what. They may be inclined to set up check sheets, attendance forms, sign-out sheets, and charts. They may want to help track inventory or anything else that needs to be accounted for.

I took it upon myself to create a closing checklist of things that need to be done before we go home for the night. My supervisor really liked it. I would rather we do something right the first time than have to do it again. If I don't have time to do it right once, when will I have time to do it again? **(ESTJ)**

I typed up an agenda for our staff meeting and also sent minutes out via e-mail (also as hard copies put in mailboxes) to hold people more accountable and remind them of their commitments. **(ISTJ)**

*I worked in the bakery of a produce shop. It was a real
small operation in the kitchen. I headed the bakery, and
there were four others making entrees and sandwiches.
Because my boss was real busy, I decided to keep track
of my own inventory and report it to him so he would not
have to figure out what bakery supplies to order for the
week. I kept track of when a new supply of baked goods
needed to be made and I came up with weekly inventory
sheets to write the count on. My boss liked that idea and
implemented his own style of the inventory sheets for his
kitchen staff.*   (ISTJ)

Theme 8: Documenting Procedures and Information

Have you ever been at a meeting where members come up with
suggestions and improvements, but no one remembers what you
all came up with? Stabilizers (especially ISTJs) tend to be careful
compilers. They can make a difference by producing handbooks,
updating information sheets, and establishing visual representa-
tions of how others will be doing their job.

*I had an externship at a family guidance agency. The
volunteers needed a handbook so that they could have
a general idea of how the child protective service system
works. So I wrote a handbook that serves as an overview
of the entire system for volunteers and new staff members
to use.*   (ESTJ)

*I can provide two examples: (1) When training a new
worker I wrote down all the main things to learn so we
could check them off together. It created the idea of a
formal training procedure (which did not exist at the time).
The increased training effectiveness allowed the new hire
to be serving the organization sooner. And (2) My manager
would leave procedure changes to word of mouth. If you*

were off for the day, no one would tell you. I put all the changes into a document on the server. Employees can now check it on their days off. They feel up to date and mistakes/misunderstandings don't happen anymore. **(ISTJ)**

My job was to do inspections of all county storm drain systems and write reports of my findings. After several years of doing this I came up with a more efficient way of collecting and storing inspection data. I implemented this new procedure on the job. At first I was told that my idea would take too much time. Now I have documented my approach and everyone has to use it. **(ISTJ)**

Theme 9: Enforcing Rules and Policies

Stabilizers (especially STJs) tend to live by the rules. They believe violators should be disciplined. They can "keep things real" by providing blunt feedback. They tend to respect authority and are willing to use their authority, albeit with a sense of fairness.

Once when I was working at a car rental agency, I had to manage a customer situation while the regular manager was gone. I was asked to explain the policy and procedure for stolen rental cars. I stated that our company does not release any rental information if the keys to the car are not with the customer. He was upset but understood it was company policy. I offered sympathy and understanding but was firm. He went to the police station. **(ESTP)**

I work at a bank and need to be cautious and really pay attention to the tasks. I caught a woman who tried to get information on an account using false ID. She wanted to withdraw a lot of money. I showed the ID to my supervisor and explained the situation. By the time I got back the lady had run away. The bank awarded me with a gift certificate. **(ISTJ)**

I was asked to sign off on some work that was not right just so the company could say they had shipped a machine. These machines were very large and took many days to test. We had to install the equipment and run a number of tests to make sure the machine powered properly. This machine did not pass the full set of tests we had to run on it. So I would not sign off on the machine despite pressure by my lead tech and my manager. They went to a different department and found someone else to sign off on the machine and it went through. People looked up to me even after that and the management took notice and said I did right. (ISTJ)

I confronted a peer who intimidated a secretary to get an appointment with their mutual boss. I let him know that I was disappointed in his behavior, especially since it impacted the secretary's self-esteem so heavily. I reminded him that we have rules about harassment. He could hardly believe that I was serious until I reviewed several of his actions and her reactions. I recommended that he come back over to speak to the secretary and try to resolve this matter before too much time passed. I volunteered to be part of the discussion. I was mainly there for support so that no intimidation would occur again. It was a revealing session that showed all three of us that our words can be misinterpreted negatively, especially when accompanied by pushy body language. This resulted in my peer becoming more careful on how he puts his words together with his body language. Our secretary has toughened up somewhat so as not to let people intimidate her and make her feel incompetent. (ISTJ)

Theme 10: Providing Task-Oriented Training

Because Stabilizers tend to be good at breaking down tasks, they can make a difference by helping orient and train new employees on the job. They can show people how to do things in a step-by-step manner. They often use their senses to observe the behavior of trainees and quiz them to verify whether they are learning. They can be good at teaching fundamentals, providing hands-on demonstrations, and working one-on-one until individuals can do it on their own.

> *I am the dining room manager at a country club. Since I train all the new employees, I am usually the first person they report to. Often they are nervous to begin, especially since we are a nice club. I recently began training a new waitress that was hired after our summer staff went back to school. She was new on the job and pretty scared. I met her at the front door and introduced myself. I walked her step by step through all of the opening routines that we go through before dinner begins. Along the way I made sure I answered all of her questions as thoroughly as possible. Once dinner began she followed me, watching every move I made. After a few tables I decided to let her have a go at it. I stood next to her making sure she did what was needed. She did an amazing job. Once we got back in the kitchen I told her how great she did. All of her previous nervousness and shyness melted away. She asked questions and wasn't nervous to try out new things. Training employees is something that I really enjoy. I like being able to help them through difficult tasks.*   (ESTJ)

> *Recently at work, I was put in charge of showing new employees around the store. I was put in charge of this situation because I have been working there for over a year and I have worked in every part of the store. When new employees come in, I take them to the four different sections and explain what they are responsible for doing on their shift. I answer any questions they have and I quiz them afterwards to see if they are ready to work a shift alone. I feel like a mentor to the new employees.*   (ESTJ)

In the past three months I have helped turn my store around.
I have trained people on how to do multiple positions. I do
this by first showing employees how to do a task. I show
them and talk them through the process as well. I find it to
be of the utmost importance to let them know why it is
necessary to do the task. Next, I watch them do it. Later,
I will quiz them on the steps of doing the operation. This
way they will be exposed to the information three different
times.   **(ISTJ)**

STABILIZERS (STs) MAKING A DIFFERENCE IN RELATIONSHIPS

Now let's look at how Stabilizers, when using the strengths of
their natural preferences, can make a difference in their personal
relationships.

Theme 1: Doing Tasks to Be Helpful

When Stabilizers see a friend or family member getting overwhelmed, it is not uncommon for them to just pitch in and do the
practical things that need doing. They can make a difference by
making plans, clarifying details, arranging schedules, or setting
up budgets for people they care about—often without even men-
tioning their being overwhelmed—in an effort to free up their
time.

My neighbor's best friend died. He was at the funeral, and I
happened to notice that his grass was really high, so I cut it
while he was gone. He got back from the funeral and real-
ized I had cut the grass for him. He was so thankful. It
allowed him to go be with the family. He respects me much
more because I helped him when he needed it.   **(ESTJ)**

I choose to do things for friends and I find it makes a
difference. I helped my sister put together scholarship

*applications, college applications, and her FAFSA form
to start college. I've developed a database for my mother
to keep track of and up-to-date with her daily daycare
activities and paperwork.* **(ESTJ)**

*Last year I noticed that one of my good friends was getting
really depressed. Everyone noticed it, but nobody seemed to
really know why. One day I was at his apartment and while
he was taking a shower I noticed a pile of bills on his kitchen
table and a list of all his debts. He was over $45,000 in debt,
and I knew this was the cause of his depression. At first I
didn't know what to do and I was really worried. Later that
week I finally got him to admit the truth to me. Once he told
me, the two of us sat down and began looking at all his bills.
Together we were able to come up with a weekly budget for
him to follow, eliminated bills he didn't have to have, such
as cable, and compiled the rest of his debt. The plan really
worked for him; he still owes $30,000 but he's working on it.
By helping him develop a financial plan I was really able to
help make a difference in his life.* **(ISTJ)**

Theme 2: Being Dependable

Stabilizers (especially STJs) can generally be counted on. They
announce their intentions and then do what they say they will.
They often develop routines in a relationship so the person they
care about will know what to expect.

*I've reduced the stress in family/friend relationships by let-
ting them know my plans and arranging specific times to
see them to show I care for them.* **(ESTJ)**

*I moved away from my sister-in-law, who I was close with,
and then we became distant. I decided to set aside a time
to call every week, Saturdays from 1 to 4, that belonged just
to us.* **(ISTP)**

I made a difference when I developed trust between my significant other and me. I did this mainly by just doing what I said I was going to do. If I wasn't sure I could do something, I wouldn't say I could. I was good at coming through on my words. Here's a small example. One time she said she wanted me to take her shopping for some clothes for a family reunion she had planned. Once I had thought to myself that I could, I told her I'd drive her that next week. It worked out great because she found what she really hoped for.   **(ISTJ)**

Theme 3: Enforcing Rules

Stabilizers (and again, especially STJs) tend to want to clarify expectations. They generally have respect for the rules as well as the history of the relationship. On occasion they may be able to keep others out of trouble.

I looked out my window one day at 6 p.m. and saw a neighbor wrestling with a guy who had a knife. Another man was in a car waiting for the person attacking my neighbor. As this was taking place, I called 911 and described the two men and their vehicle. The guys left, and I told the dispatcher the direction they took. The police caught them, and I received a citizenship award from the city.   **(ESTJ)**

At our university's basketball games, sometimes the cheer-leaders throw T-shirts into the crowd, and the people who get T-shirts get to shoot free throw baskets at halftime. At one game a T-shirt landed in a group of disabled people from a rehabilitation center. During halftime, the young man in the wheelchair who "caught" the T-shirt went to register to shoot his free throws. He came back to his seat in a very short time. I asked what happened and learned that they wouldn't let him shoot. He was quite upset. I went down out of the stands and asked the man running the con-

*test what happened. He told me he was in fear for the young
man's safety and didn't want him to make a fool of himself.
I told him that was unfair. I was then told that there was not
enough time now for the young man to shoot. So for the rest
of the night I just sat there and tried to figure out how to get
this man his opportunity to shoot baskets. The next day I
went to see the assistant vice president of the university. I
explained what went on and that I thought this was very
unfair, against the law, and that this young man should be
given the opportunity to shoot baskets at the next game. He
called the athletic director, who agreed that the young man
should be given the opportunity to shoot baskets at the next
game. So for that next Saturday, the group from the rehab
center was given free tickets to the game. When halftime
came, I went out to help the young man to the free throw
line. He was able, with some help, to stand up on this own,
and he had thirty seconds to make as many shots as he
could. He missed the first one, missed the second one, and
so on, but the crowd cheered him on every shot. The clock
read five seconds left, and with some help he put up his last
shot and it went in. The crowd went wild, and he got a
standing ovation.*   **(ISTJ)**

Theme 4: Urging Caution/Responsibility

Stabilizers tend to want to do what is right. They often push the
people they care about to finish things, to grow up, or to be careful.

*A girlfriend of mine back in high school had a best friend,
and they had an argument and kind of had a falling out.
I felt bad for both of them because I know they wanted to
talk things out but both were too stubborn to apologize. My
girlfriend never put her friend's picture away. I knew she
was still thinking about her even though she hadn't talked
to her in four or five years. I kept on her by telling her to*

give her friend a call, to grow up and realize it was a stupid argument. She finally got the nerve to e-mail her friend, who e-mailed back, and they finally got back together and reconciled their differences. (ESTJ)

My boyfriend has many big plans starting out but often has trouble following through, often because he gets bored easily. One thing I have helped to motivate him in is finishing school. He started when we first started dating and then began to take fewer and fewer classes. I've shown him the benefits of finishing school and that I would support his decision to do whatever he thought was best. I still have to motivate him every now and then, but now all I have to do is give him a little pep talk. He always tells me how much better he feels after we have talked about it and that he is glad I am there to motivate him. I am glad that I can help him. (ISTJ)

Five years ago my cousin Peter introduced me to his friend Chad. Peter and his friends were always looking for some party or place to hang out, and I found myself constantly telling them to be careful. One Friday night I had come across the boys at Peter's house and had persuaded them not to drive their cars because it was obvious they were all drunk. Apparently after I left them, Chad's other friends picked him up and took him to a party. Chad had wanted Peter and his friends to accompany these other boys, but they refused. They reminded Chad that I had told them earlier that it was not worth the risk to their lives and those of other people to drive drunk. On Saturday morning I got a call from Chad's father, who wanted me to come over to his house and talk to Chad. Arriving at the house, I saw him lying bandaged up on a bed in the living room with an IV attached to his arm. He was in a lot of pain.

The drunk driver of the SUV Chad was riding in had lost control. Chad had been ejected through the sunroof of the SUV and been dragged under the vehicle as it rolled over and skidded down the highway. Chad's father wanted to know why he was the only one that went to the party. I asked Chad why he decided to go to the party, especially with a car full of drunk teenagers. I then shared with him my experiences with drinking and driving, and reminded him that he was still young and that all the partying and fun of life would still be there after he got his education and was older and more responsible. We spoke for five hours, and Chad seemed to feel remorse. Today Chad is a senior in college and is extremely focused on his studies.

(ISTJ)

Theme 5: Dealing with Reality

Stabilizers tend to emphasize logic. They often reduce the emotionalism that is creating stress for others. By making more realistic plans and decisions grounded in reality, they sometimes reduce possible disappointment and help others avoid wasting time or money.

My son is twelve, and his mother and I are divorced. As much as my ex and I didn't get along, we have always worked hard to present a consistent, unified front to our son so he doesn't feel bounced around or have to deal with different expectations from us. We have had to put aside our feelings and deal with realities. We've had to work together to get through the problems that always come up with joint custody (for example, who our son wants to be with for holidays, vacations, and so on, and our wanting to spend more time with him). We've worked with him in sports camps, music schools, and science and activity camps over the summers and after school during the year.   (ESTJ)

A few years ago my mother and I were fighting all the time. I couldn't understand why we were fighting and I couldn't ask her without starting another argument. So one day I wrote her a letter. I explained how I felt all the arguments we had were silly and really about nothing and I couldn't understand why they kept happening. The main argument we would have was how I never came to visit, and this would always happen while I was home visiting, which in turn made me not want to come back any sooner. I felt that putting it in writing kind of took some of the emotionalism out of it. She responded with a letter of her own, and that made me realize that she was having a hard time accepting that I was becoming so independent. We came to a mutual understanding through these letters because we were able to get our own thoughts and feelings across without the other person feeling she had to interrupt to defend her side. My mom and I are now closer than ever now that we can listen to one another without feeling we are being attacked.
(ISTJ)

I once dated a girl for about three years in high school. Things became pretty serious between us, and I knew that college was right around the corner. She was more serious about the relationship than I was, and realistically I realized that my heart was not into it. I was more in it for the comfort. We had both planned on attending different universities in the fall, which would make things very difficult between us. The summer before leaving, I had decided to cut it off because it wasn't fair for the both of us to continue what really was a one-sided relationship. At times, I realize how good I had it and I miss her, but I believe that the decision I made worked out best for the both of us. She took it hard at first, but I'm sure she understands that the best logical decision was made.
(ISTJ)

Theme 6: Identifying Mistakes

Stabilizers often have the ability to use their critiquing skills to help them identify their mistakes and those of others. Often they can help others by pointing out the flaws in their thinking and by offering blunt feedback to help get them back on the right path.

I lived with my brother for two years. During that time we constantly feuded regarding my social activities, my domestic chores, and my general recklessness. However, soon after he moved out and left me solely responsible for the house, I began to recognize a lot of what he had been complaining about. As a result I quickly adjusted to a more temperate lifestyle, took a more ambitious approach to my domestic chores, and simply matured. He recently moved back into the house, and we have established a much better relationship both as brothers and roommates. **(ESTJ)**

I've been dating my current girlfriend for almost seven months now, and things have been better than great. To make one difference in this relationship, I had to try to overcome one of my own personality flaws. I have the problem of always thinking I'm right. Even when the other person (my girlfriend) talks, I don't really listen. I just wait for my turn to talk. Ever since I took her advice and started really listening, we've resolved a lot of conflict and realized I'm not always right — big surprise. Our relationship has much better communication now. **(ESTJ)**

There is a student in our class who is a new arrival to this country. I have tried to be understanding about his situation and tried to give him pointers about adjusting to life here. I have given him advice on everything from the kinds of clothes to buy, to the way to communicate with peers, to

*being careful about hygiene. People will sometimes observe
our interaction and make a comment like "Why do you
bother? . . . He'll live and learn," and to that my response is
"How is he going to learn if I don't tell him he's doing XYZ
wrong?" Not knowing where you went wrong can be a very
frustrating thing.*   (ESTJ)

Theme 7: Improving Through Small Steps

While Stabilizers tend to appreciate efficiency, they can also be
patient with others. They are generally more likely than other
types to accept slow progress and allow others to inch forward.

*One relationship situation where I feel I have made a dif-
ference is the relationship that my stepson, BJ, now has
with our family dog, Carmen. When Carmen came home,
BJ didn't really care that she was there. He spent no time
playing with her, got mad when she chewed on his toys, and
that first weekend when my husband and I had to take her
to the emergency vet, it made no difference to BJ. I started
trying to slowly include BJ in the training of this puppy.
First was teaching him to notice when to take her outside
during the potty training and how to correct her when there
was an accident. Then, helping him to teach her how to sit.
Then, instead of yelling at her when she got into his toys, to
replace the toy that she took with one of hers. Slowly, BJ
started to realize that this new puppy was a lot of fun. Now,
every night BJ calls Carmen to go in the room with him at
bedtime.*   (ESTJ)

*My son was born with cerebral palsy, and the doctors said
he would never walk, talk, or progress in school. After his
release from the hospital, his mother became hopeless about
the situation. However, I thought we should treat him like
any other kid and do everything in our power to get him the*

*resources he needed. I got custody when he was three and
that next summer I got him a walker. Within two weeks he
was walking all over with the walker. Now seven years later
he's walking on his own, doing well in third grade, and pro-
gressing at a rate that will allow him to one day take care
of himself completely. When other people were choosing
to baby him, I thought that wouldn't benefit him so I chose
to push him in a loving way, and he has been responding
beautifully.*   (ESTJ)

*I have been dating a girl who went to the same middle and
high school as I did for three years. For as long as I can
remember, she's been the only thing I'd ever wanted. Soon
after we started dating, she tells me she has an eating
problem (throws up after meals, drinks lots of water to
reduce her appetite) because she feels fat. She is 5'2" and
weighs one hundred pounds. But her drive for success and
perfection (she was a gymnast) warped her body image.
On our first date she ate a chicken sandwich, which she told
me later was a big deal. Her parents did not approve of her
eating habits and weight. It probably wasn't the right thing
to do, but I told her we'll just take a bunch of small steps.
Have a french fry, and then two and so on. As weird as it
sounds, everything turned out OK. I really think she needed
someone to believe in her and to accept her for what she
was and take things slowly with her. She still weighs around
a hundred pounds, but her appetite has increased and her
eating habits have changed for the better.*   (ISTJ)

Theme 8: Compiling Things

Stabilizers tend to want to document things. They may offer to
help others keep track of data, such as by pulling together photo-
graph albums or personal records.

I helped two dear friends who were angry at one another and were no longer talking to each other. I convinced them to come over to my house. I put together a set of videos of all the great times we shared all on one DVD. I showed this to them. They decided their friendship was worth too much to lose and apologized and forgave one another. **(ESTP)**

The biggest difference I made was in my relationship with my grandparents. They did so much for us when we were growing up, and I wanted to show them how much they mean to me. I made a scrapbook for their fiftieth wedding anniversary. I spent a lot of time going through pictures and making the perfect book with stories for each picture. I put a lot of work into it (not nearly as much as they've given us), and they were so amazed and tickled to death. It made their day even more perfect. I also did another scrapbook for them for Christmas. They're so hard to buy for, and this was something money couldn't buy. It brought back all the great times we had growing up. I know it meant a lot to my grandma because she had it scanned and about five copies made to show everyone. It was nice to know how much they appreciated it. It is something they will always treasure.

(ISTJ)

My brother's house recently caught on fire and he lost everything. The insurance is replacing all of his possessions. However, it cannot replace the sentimental value of some items. Therefore, I am collecting photos of his two children from other family members and ex-wife to scan into the computer and reprint them for him. **(ISTJ)**

Theme 9: Providing Proof

Stabilizers may enjoy digging up the facts that may convince other individuals to reconsider even personal beliefs and feelings. They may help by doing detective work or documenting the details of situations.

> *I helped a friend who was an alcoholic. He was in denial,*
> *and his problems accelerated and began to involve the*
> *law. I confronted him, but he stood firm that he had no*
> *problem. I had written down dates and events on paper*
> *he had experienced or caused and it jump-started him*
> *back into reality. It took a while, but he began to deal with*
> *his problem.*   (ESTJ)

> *I told one of my best friends that her boyfriend was cheating*
> *on her. She didn't believe me and said, "I will believe you*
> *if he would hit on you." Even though I did not have that as*
> *a goal to prove my case, sometime later he did hit on me.*
> *When I told her and even played her the messages he left*
> *on my cell phone, she broke up with him . . . but then she*
> *also never wanted to talk to me again.*   (ESTJ)

Theme 10: Encouraging Physical Activities

Stabilizers (especially STPs) may have a great love of the outdoors—for example, participating in sports such as fishing—or other physical activities. They can often add to a relationship by introducing the other person to the pleasures of such things.

> *I was married briefly to a woman whose son Brett was still*
> *in diapers when we met. I treated him like my own. He and*
> *I climbed trees, went sledding, and I introduced him to*
> *nature, fishing, and just goofing around. Unfortunately, my*
> *marriage to his mother didn't last. Then he and I didn't see*
> *or hear from each other for sixteen years. His mom called*
> *one day and we met—I didn't know he was coming—and*
> *neither of us could stop grinning. A month later I took him*
> *to a weekend paintball game. Since then we travel together*

to many states to play. My nickname on the paintball team is Dragon Man, and he picked Dragon Lad. In these paintball games I try to show by example how to play fair, follow the rules, and make new friends wherever we go. He also recently got a tattoo just like mine and in the same location. He hid it from his mom, but pride forced him to show it off.

(ESTP)

I work as a respite caregiver. When I first started taking care of Marc he was a very troubling boy. He was trying drugs and cigarettes and he was very abusive to his mother and sister. More than once I was at the home when the police brought him home. I tried taking him to baseball and basketball games, but he was not interested. We slowly learned what it took to keep his attention and things started to get better. We would go to Putt-Putt and play the games there. We also did something that some people thought was crazy: I taught him how to shoot a rifle. I trusted him, and he learned to trust me, and everything went well. When I first started taking care of him, he was in a school for violent children. After two years we were able to take him out of that school and have him put in a regular high school, and he is doing very well.

(ISTJ)

COMPARING STABILIZERS (STs) TO OTHER CORE PERSONALITY TYPES

Not only are Stabilizers not all alike, they also share some similarities with other core personality types. Generally characterized as making a difference by getting things going right away in a logical, step-by-step manner, Stabilizers share a preference for Sensing with Harmonizers (SFs—described in chapter 5). Thus both Stabilizers and Harmonizers are likely to pay attention to details, facts, and the present situation. Stabilizers are likely to do that in a manner that focuses on the task itself in a logical and objective manner, while Harmonizers are more likely to focus on the people currently involved and address situations in a more caring manner.

Stabilizers also share a preference for Thinking with Visionaries (NTs—described in chapter 7). Thus both Stabilizers and Visionaries may come across as being somewhat impersonal when trying to make a difference because they both want to analyze, critique, and logically address the situation. Stabilizers are more likely to focus on the details of the immediate situation, while Visionaries are more likely to look for patterns and interconnections among the details and seek a system that addresses the long-term issues associated with the situation.

Stabilizers generally have the least in common with Catalysts (NFs—described in chapter 6). They are likely to have a shorter-term focus and show a more practical, matter-of-fact approach to the situation, while Catalysts tend to be more idealistic.

EXERCISES FOR STABILIZERS

Before you move on to chapter 5, complete exercises 6 and 7 to help you determine how likely you are to use the themes described in this chapter to make a difference at work and in your relationships.

EXERCISE 6

Using Stabilizer (ST) Characteristics to Make a Difference at Work

Rate the extent to which you are likely to use the Stabilizer themes described in this chapter to make a difference in a work situation, on the following scale:

0 = Almost never
1 = Seldom
2 = Occasionally
3 = Frequently
4 = Almost always

continues

Exercise 6 cont'd

1. Simplifying things (produce order, schedules, plans, and short-term goals; clarify expectations; make things easier; standardize procedures)   0 1 2 3 4

2. Getting it done (push for measurable results such as cost savings, productivity, and profits; complete tasks and meetings; meet deadlines; save time and money)   0 1 2 3 4

3. Moving one step at a time (learn by trial and error; get others' buy-in with pilot efforts; encourage slow but steady progress)   0 1 2 3 4

4. Catching and correcting mistakes (double-check work; catch mistakes and prevent problems)   0 1 2 3 4

5. Just getting to work (break tasks into steps; get things started, take the initiative; take on the heavy/dirty work)   0 1 2 3 4

6. Being dependable (be loyal and reliable; show up for work; act responsibly; follow through on tasks)   0 1 2 3 4

7. Establishing accountability (know who's doing what; create check sheets, attendance forms, and so on; track inventory)   0 1 2 3 4

8. Documenting procedures and information (compile information, produce handbooks, and so on)   0 1 2 3 4

9. Enforcing rules and policies (live by the rules; provide blunt feedback; respect and use authority fairly)   0 1 2 3 4

continues

Exercise 6 cont'd

10. Providing task-oriented training (train new   0 1 2 3 4
employees in a step-by-step manner; verify
trainees' learning; teach fundamentals; provide
hands-on demonstrations; work one-on-one)

Be sure to save these ratings because you will be asked to use them in
the planning exercises in chapter 8.

EXERCISE 7

Using Stabilizer (ST) Characteristics to Make a Difference in Relationships

Rate the extent to which you are likely to use the Stabilizer themes
described in this chapter to make a difference in a *relationship*
situation, on the following scale:

0 = Almost never
1 = Seldom
2 = Occasionally
3 = Frequently
4 = Almost always

1. Doing tasks to be helpful (do practical tasks   0 1 2 3 4
to help others—make plans, clarify details,
arrange schedules, set up budgets, and so on—
to free up their time)

2. Being dependable (announce intentions; do   0 1 2 3 4
what you say you will do; develop relationship
routines; keep others out of trouble)

3. Enforcing rules (clarify expectations; respect   0 1 2 3 4
rules and history of relationship)

4. Urging caution/responsibility (do what is   0 1 2 3 4
right; push others to finish things, grow up, be
careful, and so on)

continues

Exercise 7 cont'd

5. Dealing with reality (emphasize logic; reduce emotionalism; make realistic plans and decisions based on reality)   0 1 2 3 4

6. Identifying mistakes (use critical faculties to identify and avoid mistakes; point out flaws in others' thinking; offer blunt feedback)   0 1 2 3 4

7. Improving through small steps (be patient with others; accept slow progress)   0 1 2 3 4

8. Compiling things (help others keep track of photographs, records, and so on)   0 1 2 3 4

9. Providing proof (dig up facts to change minds; do detective work; document details)   0 1 2 3 4

10. Encouraging physical activities (enjoy the outdoors, sports, physical activities; share that enjoyment with others)   0 1 2 3 4

Be sure to save these ratings because you will be asked to use them in the planning exercises in chapter 8.

How "Harmonizers" (SFs) Can Make a Difference

People with preferences for Sensing (S) and Feeling (F) tend to be very sociable and friendly, and at their core value individual relationships. We will refer to these SF types as "Harmonizers." If you have determined by looking at the middle preferences of your four-letter MBTI type that you are a Harmonizer (that is, an SF), this chapter is especially for you. You may also want to read this chapter to learn more about others who have this core personality type.

We'll start with a "scouting report" on people with this core personality type and then move to a more detailed description of these and other tendencies reported in the research studies.

Scouting Report on Harmonizers

Harmonizers tend to . . .

- Seek out and remember details about people
- Want people to be happy and will avoid conflict if at all possible
- Make decisions based on the moment and on their feelings and values
- Help make people feel included—like they belong to one big family

continues

77

Stabilizers cont'd

- Want things to be handled in a civil and respectful manner using proper behavior
- Do even impersonal tasks in a personal manner
- Come across as considerate, compassionate, loyal, friendly, and caring
- Emphasize fairness by encouraging everyone to do their fair share and live by the golden rule
- Be influenced by personal testimonials and personalized service
- Be the hosts or hostesses of the world

Overall, Harmonizers tend to make a difference . . .

- **At work** by making work, even impersonal tasks, feel more people oriented and comfortable
- **In relationships** by using their caring nature to help people feel valued and supported

A MORE DETAILED LOOK AT HARMONIZERS

Again, be sure to keep in mind that the descriptions of Harmonizers that follow reflect general tendencies only. They are not true for all people with preferences for Sensing and Feeling. Furthermore, people with any of the other three core personality types could be found to exhibit the characteristics provided in the descriptions because situations—as well as personality preferences—drive behavior. Nevertheless, in general, these descriptions will help in your understanding of the Harmonizer core personality type.

Harmonizers are generally interested in facts and details but prefer them to be about people, not things or abstract concepts. Their personal warmth exudes caring and sympathy. They are friendly types who like to help people. Many would be described as the classic "people person" and would be willing to make a sacrifice for the sake of a relationship, to please others, and at times even to try to rescue the lost soul.

They tend to approach decisions subjectively based on their personal value system. To a large extent, proof is a matter of belief to Harmonizers. They trust their feelings to determine the importance of things. As a friend or coworker, they want to know about you as a person. Harmonizers are conscientious and loyal, bringing warmth and friendliness to nearly all situations (unless the situation challenges their values). They accept people for who they are and help as many as possible feel included. They want friends to feel like family and family to feel like friends.

As providers, they give practical and personalized service, and as consumers, they want that personalized service provided to them. They want to know the specifics about how a product impacts people. They prefer to understand the world through their five senses, so they consider appearance, comfort, and clarity to be important elements of any situation. They don't want to feel pressured. Harmonizers, as their name infers, generally want to avoid conflict. They prefer civility and respect. They honor a sense of order and proper behavior.

Harmonizers would prefer to work in an organization that takes a slow but steady approach to business. They want the structure to encourage a sense of one big happy family, with many channels available for people to provide input, whether that input is in the form of facts or opinions. They generally prefer that routines be established and followed but also that personal flexibility and opinions be honored. They prefer to gather information through people, not through impersonal reports. Once Harmonizers discover something about you, it just sticks in their mind. They are likely to remember birthdays, favorite movies, and other personal information about bosses, coworkers, and customers alike.

As managers or leaders, Harmonizers are considerate, compassionate, and supportive. They emphasize fairness and dependability but are tolerant of mistakes and generally have a live-and-let-live philosophy. They go out of their way to help their people feel like they belong and facilitate interactions between staff members. They often have strong conversational skills, especially the skills that promote comfort. They value affiliation, fairness, respect, loyalty, cooperation, and the golden rule.

In work situations Harmonizers may be a bit too concerned about people. They may oversimplify problems and hold the naive belief that all people have to do is work hard and they can do anything. Because they are so open to listening to people, they are likely to know what the grapevine is saying about issues within the organization. They may get in trouble by trying to please everyone or by being self-righteous when their values are stepped on. Their decisions are sometimes influenced by personal testimonials from others, and they expect to be shown how things will benefit people they care about. It is important to them to be shown respect during any presentation.

Harmonizers contribute to an organization by being loyal participants. They help others stay focused on today's realities but with an emphasis on the people side of the business. If given the chance, they can create a warm, highly personal environment where people want to come to work. They like to apply their experience to practical jobs that support their values. They want workloads to be distributed equitably. They tend to lose interest in discussions analyzing strategic models to produce an outcome for the organization, especially if those discussions include criticisms offered in an open forum.

Harmonizers often identify with their abilities to contribute to personal relationships. They are typically more interested in these relationships with individuals than the tasks of the work itself. They genuinely care about people. The many friends of Harmonizers benefit from their warmth and support.

HOW HARMONIZERS (SFs) TEND TO DIFFER

Of course, not all Harmonizers are alike. For example, SFs who also have preferences for Extraversion and Judging (ESFJs) may tend to create an inclusive climate for their department or team in a take-charge manner. Introverted SFs (ISFs) may also generate an inclusive climate but do so by working behind the scenes. ISFs with a preference for Perceiving (ISFPs) may do so by offering numerous options. Many believe that Harmonizers tend to have an "experiencer" temperament: "Let's try things and see how we like them." The SFJs, who have a more "traditionalist" temperament, tend to prefer a more orderly approach and have a great respect for the past and for protocol.

HARMONIZERS (SFs) MAKING A DIFFERENCE AT WORK

Let's look at how Harmonizers, when using the strengths of their natural preferences, can make a difference at work. Each of the following themes represents characteristics expressed by Harmonizer participants from the research studies. Each theme is illustrated by stories written by the participants, with the storyteller's four-letter type provided at the end of each story.

Theme 1: Being There for Others

When Harmonizers are true to their nature, they can help people feel cared for, even at work. At least at first, they tend to be accepting, not judging, as they listen and provide support. They can make a difference by making coworkers feel they have someone who will be there for them in difficult situations.

> When working with clients in a helping situation (e.g., social work), before you can make a difference in someone else's life you must establish a bond or build trust with the individual or family. I soon came to realize that simply by being there and listening to everyone that I was really making a difference in their (and their family's) lives. Simply listening to this one mother in particular—to her story about why and how she came to be a resident of this community—

seemed to make a difference for her. It was clear that she was in many unhealthy and harmful relationships and situations in the past and that having someone to share her problems with, who was actually listening and willing to help, was something that rarely happened in her life. Making someone feel cared for and loved to me is the biggest and most important part of what I do. When we have staff meetings and make "mock awards" for one another, I have repeatedly been given "Most likely to be found with a child on my back or in my arms." (ESFJ)

There are many times at work that I have to deal with many different people and personalities. I am the one that everyone can talk to. Just recently a coworker of mine was in a bad relationship. This relationship was affecting his working abilities and his mental state. While I was working one night he called me and told me he was in emotional distress. I tried to talk to him and make sure he was going to make it until I could spend some time with him. I had to convince him that he wasn't at fault and he would be all right. I helped him work through this situation, and now he often thanks me for what I did and tells me I am a good person and friend. By doing this I not only made a difference at work with a coworker, but also generated a friendship.

(ISFJ)

I had a job last summer where I worked with this girl who was very insecure. She had worked there for several years and she said the people she worked with before always put her down. She said that by working with me and my sister, she actually wanted to come to work for the first time. By just being nice to her, I made her work environment more pleasant. I think that when your work environment is more pleasant to be in, you become more productive. (ISFP)

Theme 2: Being Positive

Harmonizers generally want the attitude at work to be upbeat and positive. Their optimism can be catching. At their best they are appreciative, approachable, and enthusiastic and can help create a pleasant work environment.

> *I was hired as a waiter at a local restaurant and decided to be the most positive person I could be. This attitude has helped my fellow employees understand the nature of our work. I strove to go the extra mile in helping others accomplish their tasks, encouraging others who had a harder time, and tried not to complain when things went wrong. Positivity is a major key in teams accomplishing a specific goal or task. I've encouraged others in times of discouragement. I am practical and loyal and have provided leadership in various ways by taking charge in possibly disastrous situations and following rules in times of distress.* **(ESFJ)**

> *In France I work in a leather shop. I am much younger than my coworkers and I work part-time while they work full-time. I help by generating enthusiasm, energy, and a sense of humor. I also listen well to our customers and can provide my boss with feedback about what we need to order and what the customers like.* **(ESFP)**

> *I am an assistant manager of a retail store and have been for three years now, so every day I have to display some sort of leadership qualities. When I come in to work I automatically start finding things to do, one thing at a time, and letting others know what they can do to help. Employees are always asking me what they could do or how they could do it better because they recognize me not only as an authority figure but someone they can trust. I think that is extremely*

important in a leader. The people underneath me always come to me with problems, work or personal, and they value my advice and opinions. **(ISFJ)**

There really is no hierarchy in my company. The owner of the company is everyone's boss, but after that there isn't really a pecking order. My boss is not very good at encouragement and recognition for good work. I am not a worker that needs constant positive reinforcement, but a "good job" here and there is always appreciated. Noticing this deficiency, I tend to be extra encouraging to others to make up for it. I think it makes for a more pleasant work environment if one another's accomplishments are noticed and made mention of. **(ISFJ)**

Theme 3: Being Inclusive

Harmonizers tend to help people feel like they belong. They can make a difference by being friendly. They can help set a tone that encourages people to have fun at work. Their playful spirit often shows up in the way they want to engage in team building. They may take the initiative to arrange a party or outing for the workgroup. They often make a difference by making their teammates feel included.

Our host had gotten yelled at by the manager because he's always late; he was nearly in tears. I know I hate working when I'm close to tears, so I went over to help him out. I told him, "You're not smiling because you're happy, you're happy because you smile." So I made him smile. Every time I walked past him I'd smile and make him smile too, and within the hour he was happy again. **(ESFJ)**

I currently work for a bank and have worked for this company for the past seven-plus years. My branch is not a team-oriented branch. I finally got enough courage and seniority to try to do something about the atmosphere of our bank. My first attempt was to start a Christmas party and gift exchange. The staff was all for it but then complained about having to get so-and-so a gift, and the amount of money became an issue, too. Now we individually pick a needy person's name off the Christmas tree in the lobby and give to him or her. This is a nice gesture, but it is individual, not as a team. My second attempt for team effectiveness was when I tried to talk my boss into having monthly meetings. She said she had nothing to say and doesn't like talking in front of others, but if I wanted to do this I could lead them. I decided not to because I am not the supervisor. My third attempt at team effectiveness was creating an employee birthday list and having people bring a cake in for the next person who has a birthday after theirs. This has worked! The employees actually love doing this. I keep track of the list in my computer and update when necessary. We get fattening cake usually about once a month and everyone seems to enjoy it.   **(ESFJ)**

When I began at the payroll department, my team did not really have time to train me because they were short-staffed. Another coworker, Sue, trained me. She was a member of another team but was familiar with our work. Both teams spent time, joked around, and went to lunch with their respective teams, but Sue often felt left out of both teams. When I was integrated fully into my new team, I took steps to make sure Sue did not feel left out. I stopped by her desk to talk to her, invited her to lunch, and tried to make her feel part of our team. One silly thing our team did to lighten tensions was to gently pelt each other with paper clips. While this is certainly childish, it was a bit of an inside joke and lightened everyone's mood. I took a risk and occasionally would pelt Sue with a paper clip. One day I saw a paper clip fly over the cubicle wall at me and realized it was Sue participating in our game. I think this event really signified a change in her attitude toward her coworkers and even toward the work. She seemed to be a much more positive person after that and truly felt like she was part of the team.

(ISFJ)

I created a fun spirit at work making pizzas by getting coworkers to play "I Spy" and making up mock elections and getting people to hang out with each other during lunch and after hours. **(ESFP)**

Theme 4: Getting to Know Others Personally

Harmonizers (especially ESFs) tend to want to know about the people they work with, both coworkers and bosses, on a personal level. Other people are not just a number or a title to them. They generally can help people feel like they have friends they can count on at work. They often provide personalized service to customers (and usually like to receive it when they are the customer).

I worked for a year as an educational assistant in a cross-categorical, self-contained classroom. I made the point of getting to know each student personally. Kids would come to me when they were having trouble at home or school. I did something special for each kid on his or her birthday. I also popped in on them during lunch and sent notes to them about how much I enjoyed talking with them. I visited one of "my girls" when she was admitted to a psych ward, and I also bonded with the full-time teacher assigned to the class.

(ESFP)

Now that I've started my own business I customize my clients' private gymnastics lessons to help them. I started a yoga program there for adults. One client has frequent back pain from gardening, and I aim to help her with that the most. Another client wants to tone her muscles, so I do more strength training with her. I ask both for feedback often to make sure they are getting what they need. **(ESFJ)**

I am a receptionist in a chiropractor's office. One of our patients with severe back problems always paid in cash. I helped him discover that his insurance would cover our services if he could get a referral from his primary care physician. He brought in the form at his next visit, but there were still some problems. I called over there, but that office was very disorganized. They then faxed over the wrong form. I then got on the phone and was a little rude with them because they were supposed to get the best care for their patients and they were not following through. After talking for a while we figured out they needed some more information from us. I found it and faxed it to them. By the end of the day, our patient had a referral to cover sixty visits. I called the patient and told him what happened. He was very happy, and the next time he came in he was singing my praises to my boss. **(ISFP)**

I work in the radiology department of a hospital. One day an elderly patient was brought in for an X-ray by her daughter. The patient was ninety-two years old and in a wheelchair, and her daughter was on crutches. When the patient's exam was done, I noticed the daughter struggling to use her crutches and push her mother in the wheelchair at the same time. I offered to push the wheelchair out to the daughter's car. As we were making our way out to the parking lot, they realized they also needed to stop at the pharmacy. I pushed the patient to the pharmacy and stood waiting for her to get her prescriptions. The daughter said that she could push her mother the rest of the way because it would be a while before her pills were ready. I said don't worry about how long it takes, I can wait. After twenty-five minutes' wait I helped the mother into her daughter's car. They were both so grateful and could not thank me enough. Even though it is not my job to transport patients, I am always glad to lend a helping hand.   (ISFJ)

Theme 5: Being Respectful, Behaving Properly

Harmonizers often display a natural tendency for civility. They want people treated fairly and equally. They can make a difference by advocating the golden rule. Their sense of values and ethics helps colleagues feel they are in a workplace that has integrity. If they should happen to tease others for fun, they may quickly apologize—they don't want to offend anyone. They can help establish an expectation of proper behavior.

One of the guys on our ship made a racial comment/joke. He was new and probably just trying to impress his new shipmates. Being the leading petty officer, it was up to me to correct his behavior. There is no room in the military for comments like this. Equal opportunity and respect for every person is the working environment we must provide. I was torn on exactly how to handle the situation. Should I counsel him in private, or make an example out of his behavior? I did the latter, explaining that tasteless or racial jokes will not be tolerated in our work spaces. Everyone around agreed with me, and this helped cement the point and hopefully built some positive peer pressure. I never heard another inappropriate comment from him again.   (ESFP)

In my current job I maintain that a returning employee was being rude and unhelpful to a new employee. The old employee would always talk about the new employee while he was not there. One day I just told off the old employee, but I was still polite. I just let him know he should not talk

*about people while they were not around to defend them-
selves and that he should concentrate more on doing his
job and helping his fellow employees get adjusted and stop
criticizing them for the little mistakes they made. He should
use that energy to teach them the right way. I also encouraged the new employee to stand up for himself and not let
people treat him any way they feel like. The new employee
addressed the issue to our boss, and now the returning
employee is a lot more helpful and nicer to new employees.*

(ISFJ)

*A few years ago, my boss hired a girl that was in high school.
I would only work with her a couple of times a week, but I
thought there was something shady about her. I couldn't put
my finger on it right away. However, the more I paid attention to her when we worked together, the more I noticed how
nervous she acted. Well, one day some of her friends came
in and she didn't know that I was upstairs. I watched her
give them a ton of free candy and slushes. I didn't say anything to her; I just told my boss, and she was fired right
away. We still don't know how much she stole, but she
worked at the store for about four months.* (ISFP)

Theme 6: Smoothing Conflict

SFs are labeled Harmonizers because they would rather not have
conflict in their life. They tend to be accommodating and may
avoid even raising issues that could produce conflict. This, they
feel, reduces stress and makes work more comfortable for themselves and others.

*At the fire department, I am usually the one who is settling
people's differences. For example, two people were arguing
over an issue that was starting to get heated. I immediately
stepped in and said, "OK, both of you go to your corners to*

cool off for a minute." I was then able to ask each person the facts to their side of the story without the added yelling or sarcasms. I then described two scenarios of a win-win outcome. Both parties were able to resolve their disagreement and walk away feeling good and keeping a relationship with the other.   **(ISFP)**

I have smoothed things over when people at work expressed their views on a variety of topics (for example, the NRA) and got into heated arguments. I pointed out that everyone is entitled to their opinion and also mentioned why different people may think and feel the way they do. I am always upbeat and positive and make people laugh.   **(ESFP)**

My coworker and I have to work with three very lazy people who are never pushed/reprimanded to work harder. I noticed we've started complaining almost the whole eight hours we work together. Knowing this doesn't help, I tried to lighten the workplace by bringing in my CD player. It helped. We have more discussions about music and other stuff when it's there. This makes the workplace more pleasant.
                                                                (ISFP)

When I first started my position I felt quite intimidated because I, the supervisor, am much younger than the employees that I am supervising. I wanted people to like me, but also to take me seriously as a supervisor. Not long after starting, a new food service employee named Faith was hired. She has a very different personality than I do. It was not long before our personalities started to conflict. She is very abrasive in her speech and basically says what she wants to without thinking of the consequences. On one occasion, Faith was very rude to me. I was pretty upset, so I discussed the situation with my supervisor, who then held a meeting with Faith and me. This actually made the situation

*worse. Faith would not speak to me and gave me dirty looks
for the next few weeks. I regretted telling my supervisor
about the event. Gradually, Faith got over the episode, as
did I. We both seemed to make a fresh start. Now we have
a better understanding of each other, which makes our
relationship stronger. I still do not agree with some of
Faith's conduct, but I am willing to give her the benefit of
the doubt. I often do not take what she says to me too seriously because I understand her personality better than I did
in the beginning.* (ISFJ)

Theme 7: Showing Loyalty to the Organization

Harmonizers tend to show gratitude. They are typically dedicated
to their organization but especially to the people they work for.
Their loyalty often shows up in their willingness to volunteer.
Unless they feel they have been wronged, they are likely to make
a difference by being committed, or at least compliant.

*There was a girl that was let go at my current job. Basically,
she packed up and left without telling our boss she was
leaving. So I was the one to tell my boss. I told my boss that
I would go through her desk, figure out what needed to be
done, and then do it myself. My boss just looked at me and
said, "You are a lifesaver." She also told me she wouldn't
know what to do if I wasn't there.* (ISFJ)

*In 2004, we had heavy thunderstorms that knocked out the
power to our whole area. After making sure my family was
safe and sound, I went to the hotel where I work and helped
get flashlights to guests, contacted sources to get our power
restored, and coordinated with power company employees
who helped with tree removal. Our computer system had to
be backed up from the previous night's tapes. That meant
we had to redo all the work from that morning on. I helped*

reenter everything manually, checked the correct form of payment for everyone who departed that day, verified which rooms were actually vacant or occupied, all on one of the three busiest days of the whole year. Then I had to play catch-up with the third shift audit, finally finishing up about twelve to fourteen hours later.   **(ISFP)**

I had always wanted to work at this lotions and fragrances company from the first time I set foot in the store. As soon as I turned eighteen, I applied to work there. My very first day on the job, I took the initiative to start pulling product from the back room. I filled the shelves and understocks. The boss was so amazed by my hard work and determination. He pulled me to the side after my shift to talk to me. I hoped that I was not in trouble for just going ahead and working without asking someone what to do. He told me, "I have worked for twenty-two years in retail and I have NEVER had an associate walk onto a job the first day and take the initiative to work nonstop like you did today." I always felt like I was a very hardworking and determined employee. That day, my boss confirmed what I believed to be true about myself.   **(ESFJ)**

My manager at work called me on a Wednesday afternoon and she was crying. Her nephew had been severely injured at a Fourth of July outing. She needed me to come and work for her so she could go to the hospital. This was a day that I had school all day and dance class at night. I felt the need to help her out and put off my day so she could go to the hospital. Also, the next day I brought her ice cream to cheer her up.   **(ESFJ)**

Theme 8: Rescuing Individuals

Harmonizers genuinely care about others. For example, if a colleague has been treated unfairly by the organization's bureaucracy, they may be willing to go to bat for that person despite their dislike of conflict. Their generally accepting nature makes them likely to try to rescue "lost souls," and they often cheer for the underdog. They can make a difference at work by helping create a kinder, gentler, fairer organization.

> *A new employee, Lucy, who just finished the two-week training program, was sent to my branch to work with me as her mentor. We got this girl four months ago; at first she didn't seem to catch on to anything. All the other tellers were telling the managers how bad she was doing and that she wasn't going to make it as a teller. The manager approached me and asked what I thought, because I was the one working with her. I asked if she and I could stay one night after we closed and I could work with her, with no one else to bother us. The manager agreed. So one night Lucy and I stayed after work for about three hours and worked in the training room. I just explained to her that I know all of the information she received was overwhelming and all she had to do was take her time and slow down and read the computer screen before she did a transaction. The screen tells you what you are going to need to process the transaction and what to point on. It was very simple. The next day, she ran a window all by herself and felt confident. I told the managers she would do fine, just give her another week or so. Everyone else doubted Lucy from the beginning, but no one took into consideration that all of us have been tellers for five-plus years. All she needed was a little extra coaching and someone to tell her she could do it, instead of giving her all the negative feedback. Now Lucy is doing great and is having no problems keeping up with the rest of us.*   **(ESFJ)**

> *I was a manager for the movie theater at the mall (at age eighteen) and had to deal with a variety of employees, from teenagers (my peers) to individuals with special needs. As*

many tend to do, the teenagers ridiculed the special-needs ones (or, as they nicknamed them, the "Dream Team"). One employee, Jarrell, in his mid to late twenties, was a key player on the Dream Team. He thought he was quite the ladies' man with female employees at other stores. Jarrell was obviously impaired—clear even to a child. I was curious why these young girls were so willing to spend time with someone they were also so quick to mock. I found out Jarrell was giving them money. He would buy them whatever they wanted, such as food and free movies. I couldn't tell Jarrell and break his heart, so I approached these girls and banned them from the theater and threatened to talk to their managers. They stayed away for fear of losing their job. Unfortunately, when I returned to work the other employees had convinced Jarrell to dress up in an evening gown covered in sequins, plus high heels and costume jewelry, while singing "I Will Survive" by Gloria Gaynor. I talked to Jarrell in the back room and asked him to check with me before doing anything else our coworkers suggested. I then held a meeting of the other employees and asked them to take the high road. I insisted they treat Jarrell as they would like to be treated. Occasional comments continued, but overall things got better, and to my knowledge Jarrell was not singled out for humiliation at work again. (ISFP)

Theme 9: Providing Comfort

Harmonizers tend to be caring types, very much in tune with physical sensations. Thus it is not unusual for them to be concerned with comfort, aesthetics, food, and other elements of the physical setting at work. Others may find they benefit from Harmonizers' natural interest in having good lighting, nice furnishings, and other comforts of home in the workplace.

In each job I try to make the whole environment or atmosphere welcoming and warm for both customers and employees alike. I think it is important that people feel comfortable. I go the extra mile to help someone out or to make the place look inviting. **(ESFP)**

I found out where to order headsets for the appointment administrators, who are on the phone constantly throughout the day. This helped reduce complaints of neck pain and helped free up their hands for typing and paperwork. **(ISFJ)**

I worked on a school improvement team. Our goal was to develop ways in which we could make improvements within the school system. I was a student representative; I gave a perspective and worked with parents and teachers to cooperatively make decisions. I encouraged our team to focus on how to beautify school grounds and buildings, how to make high school less competitive, and how to make sure everyone can take part in school activities such as float building, sports, and organizations. **(ISFP)**

One day my manager was having an awful day and was extremely stressed. I got her favorite candy and a coffee, and we sat down and talked about anything other than work. **(ESFP)**

Theme 10: Creating Order

Harmonizers often try to create a sense of order in the workplace—cleaning, filing, making checklists and to-do lists, and so on—in a friendly manner. They tend not to start with a grand plan; they just start organizing things. They generally prefer a clean, safe environment, with everything in its place.

When I applied for my current job, I found the office very unorganized. It was a total mess, and you felt like you would keep bumping into things. I don't think people like to work in messy environments. Well, one day when my boss was out for a meeting, I decided to go ahead and take the initiative of cleaning out the back room. You are supposed to ask the manager if you can do certain things. I just went ahead and did it, which is a bit unusual for me. This project was an all-day job. My boss came back early that afternoon and saw what I had done. She said that the room has never been cleaned and organized like that from the day she started working thirty years ago. By organizing and cleaning the room, it has made things much more pleasant and efficient for us. We know exactly where things are, and things are labeled so we don't spend so much time looking for them. (ISFJ)

We were having a problem at work. Basically the girls were getting upset with having to clean up the mess left behind from the whole department. I work in jewelry, and a lot of little things end up lying around. Before you know it, you have piles of messes. Well, everyone was leaving it. They felt, "Why should I have to clean up if no one else does?" So I separated the mess into shoeboxes. Each person was responsible for getting through a box each day. By doing this it gave them an individual goal to focus on. I then gave rewards after the boxes had been completed. They later told me that they really liked the idea. Eventually, on their own the girls would go and fill their box up with jewelry pieces that needed to be put back, damaged out, and pieced together. Management congratulated me on the idea and was thankful. When inventory came around we were 100 percent more prepared than the year before. (ISFJ)

When I first started working, the place had a BAD filing system—like important documents were missing, signatures were missing, and so on. My first day there, they showed me where they kept the residents' files and they showed me the

huge stacks everywhere. I thought to myself, I know their fil-
ing system should be better than this. So, once I pretty much
figured out where everything went, including the order of the
documents, what color folder each resident needed (because,
depending on their income, that determined the folder color,
and I think it was four colors), I had a system going. Filing
is way my thing! I think it took me almost three weeks to
catch them up because the filing was backed up for months.
The ladies in the office trusted me when it came time for
audits. We always get good feedback because I made sure
that those files were as close to perfect as possible.   **(ISFP)**

HARMONIZERS (SFs) MAKING A DIFFERENCE IN RELATIONSHIPS

Now let's look at how Harmonizers, when using the strengths of their natural preferences, can make a difference in their personal relationships.

Theme 1: Being There for Others

People with whom they have a close relationship are typically very important to Harmonizers. They are often willing to drop what they are doing and be there for those they care about. They pro vide nonjudgmental support, accepting people for who they are. They listen and care, and they help people feel OK and not alone in the world.

A long time ago, when I was sixteen, my best friend found
out she was pregnant. We went to the drugstore together
and bought the test and returned to my house, where she
took it. It immediately turned positive, and she started
to cry. I just comforted her until I decided that it would
probably be better if I told my mom. She would have a
better idea of how to handle the situation. We all talked

about the roads she could take, and we laughed, cried, and bonded. My mother even offered that she would adopt the child and my friend could always see her. Looking back at it today my girlfriend says that was when she knew that we were life-long friends. The moment my family stepped up and became her family too. We still talk about the situation, but those few hours we spent together that day had the most impact on our relationship up until this point.   **(ESFJ)**

Last semester one of my best friends' grandfather died. I've known her since we were both in kindergarten, so I knew his situation and that he had been struggling for a while. My friend was studying in Spain at the time. I went to the view-ing at the funeral home so I could give my condolences to her family. When I told her that I had gone, she told me that it meant a lot to her since she couldn't be there. I always want my friends and family to know that I am there for them, because that is what I think the whole point of having good relationships is: that you can have someone you can count on to be there during good times and bad and know that they can help you through it.   **(ISFJ)**

I had a friend who was struggling with his sexuality. He knew he was bisexual but felt he could not come out, being afraid of what others would think. Another close friend and I spent a lot of time with him and showed him enough respect that he felt comfortable enough to come out to us. We knew nine months before anyone else. We showed him that people had the compassion to accept him for who he is and to not judge him. It was a great comfort to him to know he had true friends that accepted him unconditionally.
(ISFJ)

My best friend's parents were getting divorced, and she had just found out. She was very upset, so I went and stayed the entire weekend with her while her father moved out. It was very hard because she was so upset. We were up most nights due to her not being able to sleep. As I got ready to go back home she thanked me for staying with her and told me I made it a little easier for her.   **(ISFP)**

Theme 2: Offering Encouragement

Harmonizers tend to offer more than simply passive support to the other person in a relationship. They offer encouragement. They can make a difference by helping others believe in themselves.

My husband Jeff and I have a very trusting and strong relationship. We have wonderful communication and thoroughly enjoy being each other's best friend. Jeff's background is completely opposite of mine. He did not finish high school—his parents let him drop out. After he got his GED, they never encouraged him to go to college. They never told him what a wonderful person he is and that he could be anything he wanted in life. They never congratulated him when got an A in his first college class. They never ask him how his brand-new house is, or tell him how proud they are that he is such a responsible adult. They have not supported or motivated him in all of his twenty-nine years.

I decided one day I needed to influence Jeff's thinking into a more positive mode. For one week I told him every day how handsome he is, and by the end of the week he was telling me, "Hey honey, I look pretty good today." I could tell that his self-esteem was increasing. Next, I decided to encourage him to pursue his dreams, because he could be anything he wanted to be. His true dream was to become a state police officer—funny, that's what my dad is. I encouraged him to sign up for some college classes and take the exam. He did. In his first college course he earned an A and loved all of the knowledge he was gaining; he still continues to take classes. In the past six years I have watched my husband develop into a person who believes in himself. Jeff is a hard worker and good person who appreciates life and never takes it for granted. I am very proud to have him as my husband and am glad that I might have made a difference in his life with positive encouragement and motivation.   **(ESFJ)**

I made a difference in a relationship when I coached youth hockey. This young man, Ryan, possessed a lot of talent but lacked desire and needed to be pushed and encouraged. In practice we would go through several conditioning and skill drills. I had been noticing that he was taking these drills lightly and going through the motions. I decided that I would challenge him by skating alongside him and make comments to get him going. I even pulled him aside to talk to him and make sure everything was right in his life. I also explained the importance of doing the drills as hard as he could, because that's the only way he would improve. Mid-way through the season I noticed that he was really working hard in the practices as well as the games and he was starting to notice improvements in himself. The reason I know that I made a difference in this young man's life was the responses to his personal profile sheet. Each player filled out a sheet that listed specific information, and this book was then sent out to all of the college coaches. One of the questions on the profile sheet was to indicate your current hockey idol. Ryan's response to this question was my name. Most of the other players listed Steve Yzerman and Wayne Gretzky.   **(ISFJ)**

Theme 3: Verbalizing Feelings

Harmonizers (especially ESFs) will generally let you know how they feel. They are open and encourage others to be so, too. They express their feelings in a direct and matter-of-fact manner but are

mostly polite—unless they are upset. They can help make a difference in a relationship by making sure that feelings on either side
aren't all bottled up.

> *I have the utmost respect for my dad. He is a very logical
> man. He looks at problems from an objective, sensible, and
> rational perspective. I always have had respect and admira-
> tion for my father and his decision-making skills. However,
> somewhere along the way I began to just do whatever my
> dad's opinion was and not what I wanted to do. He never
> said, "This is what you have to do," but I just always did
> what he thought I should. Sometimes later I would get
> angry because I did not want to do what I was doing or
> because I did not like the results of the decision I had made.
> I have learned from this experience and others that I have
> to have an idea or an opinion before I talk to my father. This
> makes us have more of a two-sided conversation rather than
> me just listening and agreeing. This has made a positive
> difference in our relationship.*   **(ESFP)**

> *I am dating someone now who is a little bit older than me
> and has not dated for quite some time. He was previously
> dating a girl for quite some time and he was hurt badly by
> her. I think I have made a difference in the following ways.
> First, I encourage him to say things that he normally wouldn't
> say. When we first started dating he was very closed with
> his feelings, and lots of times I would have no idea what he
> was feeling or if he was angry with something or anything
> else for that matter. Now he is more open with his feelings
> because I have showed him that he can trust me with his
> feelings and that I really respect him and what he has to
> say. No matter what he says to me, he knows that he will
> not be laughed at and that I won't think anything he says
> is silly or unimportant. I also try to generate a little enthusi-
> asm from him, too. He was very leery about being some-*

body's boyfriend again, but now he gets very excited to say that he is dating someone, and he has been told that he "glows" when talking about me. This makes me feel good also, knowing that he is excited to be in a relationship again, and it shows me that I am doing my part to help this relationship be a successful one.   **(ISFJ)**

My mom recently started dating, and my sister and I have been very uncomfortable with the situation. My mom and I have been on speaking terms, but things are very awkward. My sister and my mom weren't talking at all. My mom suggested that we all sit down and talk, and I agreed. My sister on the other hand didn't want to discuss anything. I talked with her and told her that our mom was trying to make an effort to resolve things and that I'd really appreciate it if she'd have the talk. She decided to do it, and although it was very emotional and awkward, everything got out in the open and things are a lot better now.   **(ISFJ)**

Theme 4: Being Loyal

Harmonizers tend to be trusting. They generally want a sense of togetherness and help family and friends feel a sense of belonging. They can make a difference by being loyal to others.

I made a difference in a relationship when I decided to be a friend to a five-year-old, Austin. This kid came from a broken family and lived with his father. His father worked a lot to pay the bills, so Austin would often go with his aunt to her cottage on Rose Lake, next door to my grandma's house.

Austin took a liking to me right away. He needed someone to be his friend. I decided that I didn't mind doing that. First we went swimming. He was just learning how to swim, so he was a little afraid of the water. I got him a life jacket out of the shed and put it on him. We swam around for a while, then I began to teach him how to swim right. He was

afraid, but he trusted me. Next I took him fishing. He had
never been fishing, but off we went and caught some
bluegills and other pan fish. The look on his face when he
caught his first fish was amazing. I loved it! We could have
spent all day fishing. Basically what I did was be nice to a
kid. It was easy to do. I just spent time with him. We played,
swam, fished, roasted marshmallows, went looking for deer,
and other little things. I made a friend for life. Every time I
see him I get a big hug hello and another one when I leave.
It is special. **(ESFJ)**

My husband has two adult daughters from a previous mar-
riage. There are only a few years between their ages and
my own. Before my husband and I knew each other, he had
very little contact with his kids. Since we have been together
his oldest daughter has come for visits several times from
Florida and has told me that if it wasn't for me she would
not come. His youngest daughter calls infrequently but
before she didn't call at all. The oldest daughter called a
few weeks ago with some disturbing news about her son—
she wanted me to break it to my husband. I did, and after
he had time to digest the news they had a rational conversa-
tion about it. The daughter called the other day to tell me
she and her sister were planning a surprise visit at Christmas
and wanted me to pick them up at the airport. I don't take
credit for these relationships, but I think my presence helps
create an access for enhancing them. **(ESFJ)**

My dad has three other daughters besides myself. Unfortu-
nately, they aren't very close and they don't talk much at all.
My dad can't even remember the last Father's Day any of
them spent with him. Two years ago on Father's Day I was
going to try to make a difference. I planned a get-together
and sent out invitations. I thought it would be nice if my
dad could be with all of his daughters for at least one

Father's Day. Well, unfortunately it didn't happen. Only one of his other daughters was able to make it. I guess one is better than none, and my dad was happy. I still wish the other two had come.   **(ISFP)**

When visiting friends in Lebanon, I met a girl that I started to like. However, I noticed that my best male friend seemed to be upset by this. I couldn't understand because he already had a girlfriend. I found out that he was hoping to break up with his girlfriend and start seeing this other girl. I analyzed the situation and decided that since I was soon to be returning to the U.S., I would keep my relationship with the girl as just a friend. I chose loyalty to my friend rather than feelings of lust. When my male friend noticed this, our friendship was quickly restored.   **(ESFP)**

Theme 5: Making Others Happy

Harmonizers tend to feel that life should be fun. They smile and generally get others to smile, too. They make a difference by being thoughtful in many ways, such as by sending flowers and cards on special occasions or just to say they care. They often provide affection and verbal expressions of love. They sometimes help others by smoothing hurt feelings and offering statements of appreciation. At their best they make a difference by providing comfort and other acts of kindness.

One way I make a difference with my friends is that I frequently give cards for no particular reason. I find myself migrating toward the "blank inside" card aisle when I go grocery shopping. Sometimes I send my boyfriend text messages, when I know he is stressed out or is working all day, that say something like "Smile, someone is thinking of you." Whether or not this really makes a difference, I try. One way I try to make a difference in my relationship with my mom is that, sometimes when I go home when she is sleeping (during the day, since she is a nurse and works nights), I will leave her flowers on the table downstairs to make her smile when she comes downstairs. I know that her job is very stressful. **(ESFJ)**

I made a difference in a relationship with a man who is now my husband. This is the second marriage for both of us, and he tells me how happy I make him feel. I try to make things easy for us. He says he never realized that relationships could or should be easy. He always thought they had to be difficult and challenging. That made it tough for us at first, but I continued to be myself—being affectionate, making things fun, caring for him as a person—and we fell in love. He now likes the "sappy" things I do (flowers, food, music, pretty things, and especially the caring), and I like how he cares about our future and how much he gives at work, to friends, and to family. We are two quite different people but we have made a great life for us together. It turns out we share core values that weren't obvious at first. **(ESFP)**

I live in a small town, and every Christmas the streets are lit up with candles in white bags. I volunteer to place bags and candles all over town. One year we went out early in the morning, when we should have been sleeping in and not freezing. We went to some homes of elderly people and set the lights up so they could see them through their windows. We placed them around the schools to show that students do care about the town and to show appreciation for the tradition. That day I realized what the town does to extend the Christmas cheer. The whole town becomes one shining light. Every road, inlet, and house has these candle bags, and it completes the tradition. It feels great to do this with my friends and feel we are making a difference. **(ISFP)**

In my family I have made a difference because I am always the expressive one. I am the first one to give hugs and tell everyone that I love them. Even when I was real young I was very affectionate. My grandma used to call me "cuddle bug." I think it is because I am so affectionate that my family is closer to each other. **(ISFP)**

I am nurturing by nature. So if someone is sick, I will bring them soup; or if someone needs a ride someplace, I will gladly take them. For instance, last week my boyfriend came down with the flu, so I brought him soup, ginger ale, and stomach antacid to make him feel better. **(ISFJ)**

Theme 6: Rescuing Others

Harmonizers can be a real sucker for lost souls. The good news is that they have rescued many an underdog. They have been known to help friends and family members escape from abuse. Harmonizers can make a difference by accepting those who may have been excluded elsewhere and give them a sense of belonging.

A guy in my school was put in jail. His mom said he had hit her (which we found out later, too late, wasn't true). His dad is not in the picture, and he didn't have any friends. I visited him in jail every Tuesday for three months and found him a place to stay when he got out. He's doing good now.

Another guy I met was also put in jail. He was not supposed to leave the county but he ended up here. His parents refused to talk to him, and all his friends are still back home, without a clue where he is. I see him Mondays and Fridays and go to his court dates if they don't interfere with class time. When he gets out in February (maybe sooner) he will have a place to stay, and I've talked to his boss (where he was working when he was locked up), and he is guaranteed a job when he gets out. **(ESFJ)**

I had a friend with an alcohol problem. He was an amazing athlete but had two DUIs before he was 21. He became vio-lent and dropped out of college. I was part of an interven-tion with his friends and family, and we got him into rehab and counseling. When he got out, I never drank with him and tried to help keep him focused on being sober. He has been sober for a year (aside from a few setbacks). He is back in school and is doing much better."   **(ESFP)**

My roommate of three years dated a guy she met here at college. He was a baseball player, and she's a gymnast. They dated for quite some time, but he then became very control-ling and angry with her. The yelling turned to physical abuse, and she did not know how to get out of the relation-ship because they had dated for so long. I then talked with her about it, and together we set up an appointment with a program that helps abused women get themselves out of that kind of situation. After a week of meetings, she finally built up the courage to leave him, and I went with her to get her things and tell him that she was through with him. She then thanked me for helping her schedule the meetings and supporting her through this abusive relationship.   **(ISFP)**

Once in a while I would get phone calls at 3 a.m. from a friend who was very troubled. He was about nineteen years old and was unhappy with his life. A few times he was suici-dal. I would get out of bed and drive an hour to be with him and calm him down. I would ask him about what was going on in his life and ask him why he was so unhappy. Then I would offer my advice. Most of the time he would listen, but there would be those few times that he wouldn't and I would receive more phone calls. We lost contact for some time, about eight months. And then I ran into him at a club. He introduced me to his friends and told them that I was the

reason he was standing there, and if it wasn't for me he
would be dead.   **(ISFJ)**

Theme 7: Hosting

Harmonizers (especially ESFs) tend to like to host parties and
events. They often help their significant others, friends, and family members feel included and comfortable. They can remember
things about other people and can be particularly good at connect-
ing individuals to one another.

> *Recently my mom's family came to America to live, and my*
> *cousins who grew up in India needed help getting settled in*
> *their new place. This is a huge move. India and America are*
> *very different—for instance, the culture and traditions, and*
> *a big difference is the language. When they got here I helped*
> *them with many different things. First I took them shopping*
> *to get them clothes that are trendy, so when they start high*
> *school they won't feel like outcasts. (I know high school stu-*
> *dents can be very rude and foolish.) Also, I helped them with*
> *their English; they knew how to read and speak it but they*
> *still needed some help. My sister and I also showed them*
> *around, took them out, and introduced them to our friends*
> *so they would not feel left out or lost.*   **(ESFJ)**

> *Once I heard one of my neighbors say that the people who*
> *live in our building really don't care about other neighbors.*
> *This comment made me start thinking, and I thought that,*
> *yes, what he was saying was true, but the cause of this was*
> *that we, as neighbors, didn't have a close relationship with*
> *each other. So I got the idea to make a reunion at my apart-*
> *ment for all the neighbors in order to get to know a little bit*
> *more about each one of them. I planned and I distributed*
> *the invitations, and the reunion happened. Almost all of the*
> *neighbors assisted, but they were wondering what the real*
> *reason was for that reunion. I told them the story that moved*

me to do it, and after this first reunion the relationships among the neighbors has improved. Now all of us know each other and care in some positive way about each neighbor. **(ISFJ)**

I've made a difference in my friend Michelle's life. One example is that I threw her a surprise twenty-first birthday party. I invited so many people—mostly from our church— and her mom invited her family and family friends. We ended up having a great turnout, and Michelle was completely surprised! Later she told me that she was worried that she wouldn't have a memorable twenty-first birthday. Then she thanked me for making it memorable for her.

(ISFJ)

The biggest role I play with friends is connector. I really don't try to make a big difference, but a lot of my friends that now party together would have never met if they hadn't hung out with me. Whether it was a party I hosted or a gathering at the bar, I think I'm responsible for at least a dozen ongoing relationships. **(ISFJ)**

Theme 8: Smoothing Conflict

Conflict tends to make Harmonizers uncomfortable. If their friends or family members are feuding, they may be willing to play the role of peacemaker. They often offer forgiveness and encourage others to do so as well. They can smooth ruffled feathers in a way that makes a difference.

Once at a bar in Seattle, I was with five friends from my navy days and having a good time. However, one of the guys was within one comment of getting into a big fight with another patron of the bar. I stepped in and told my friend to go to another part of the bar. I told the other guy that we were in the navy and that my friend missed his girlfriend really bad. The guy understood and told me to tell my friend to just not talk to his girlfriend (who was standing right next to him). Everything was cool, and I even got a free drink out of the deal. (ESFP)

I have resolved a major conflict in my family before. When I was in third grade one of my aunts and uncles stopped talking to the rest of my family because of something another aunt of mine said. This went on until I was in seventh grade. I was so sick of no one in my family stepping up to try to fix the situation, and I didn't want my grandma to pass away with her kids not talking to each other, so I decided to step up. Around my cousin's eighteenth birthday (he was a part of the family that wasn't talking to us), I made him a birthday card and wrote a letter to him. I said that I still loved them and that I hoped that sooner or later we could start talking again. I then rode my bike up to a mailbox and sent it without anyone knowing what I had done. About a week later my mom and dad stopped me to ask if I had sent Matt (my cousin) the card and letter. I said yes, and they told me that we were invited to his graduation party. As the years have gone by, my family has gotten closer to my aunt and uncle again. Before she passed away, my grandma knew that everything was getting better. I look back and smile when I think that it took a twelve-year-old to get the family to talk again. (ISFJ)

My fiancé has always had a bad relationship with his biological father because his father left him and his mother very early on in life and he holds this against him. Since we are now planning our wedding, I suggested that he may want to notify his father that he is getting married. He finally picked up the phone and called his father to let him know about our wedding. My fiancé was quite hesitant but he put his feelings aside for me and our wedding. They spoke for the first time in years without fighting with one another, and as a result of this conversation we meet with him once a month for dinner to catch up with one another.

(ISFP)

When my friends get into arguments, I like to break the ice with a joke to get them to talk again. When my coworkers are down or sad, I tell them a funny story or situation to help cheer them up. When I argue with my friends I usually am the first to say I'm sorry.

(ISFJ)

Theme 9: Advocating Values

Harmonizers generally make decisions based on their values. They have a sense of right versus wrong and tend to encourage and appreciate proper behavior. Their beliefs and faith can serve them as they make a difference in relationships.

When I was eighteen, I attended Northern Michigan University. One day, while I was visiting home, my father, who lives in the Upper Peninsula and is a post commander for the state police, asked me if I would be interested in conducting a "sting" operation. The operation consisted of buying alcohol from local merchants in a nearby town who sold to minors. I was then a criminal justice major at NMU and felt it would be a beneficial experience. I attempted to buy alcohol at thirteen stores; eight did sell to me. I could not believe how easy it was, even though I did not look mature for my age at eighteen.

A few months after the sting operation was over, my dad subpoenaed me, and I had to go in front of the Liquor Control Commission and recall my experience. The people of the community who were affected were very angry with me and tried to intimidate me. But those who had children my age were very appreciative that the state police took some action and brought some attention to the problem of underage alcohol purchasing. I hope that I saved some lives of teenage kids who drink and drive or drink themselves to death. I might have really upset the ones that were caught, but the percentage of good to bad doesn't even compare.   **(ESFJ)**

In February 1999, I met Angela, the girl who is now my wife. We had no clue where we were going to end up. Being Albanian, she could not date at all. Angela went behind her family's back to have this friendship with me. After about six months, I realized she was the fantasy girl I wanted as a wife. She had developed feelings for me. From that time until November 2000 we never went on dates or did any-thing besides talk on the phone and e-mail each other. The only time we saw each other was at church, where we could not even act like we knew one another. Around June of 2000 we talked about marriage and how I would go and ask for her hand in marriage. In late July I went to Europe and didn't return until late August.

Things had changed during the time I was gone. Her father was pressuring her to get married because many men were asking for her hand in marriage. Her father didn't understand why she didn't want these men when they had such a good family and were smart and successful. In our culture that's what things were based on. All this happened at a bad time for me because of school and football. In Sep-tember, a boy who her father got attached to clearly asked her for her hand. He was hard on her because of him. She kept refusing, so I had to make the decision. Should I marry her? I didn't finish school; I didn't have any degree. As you know, I made up my mind and asked for her hand in mar-riage. I saved this girl from marrying someone she didn't know. Things turned out well.   **(ESFJ)**

Theme 10: Sacrificing for Others

It is generally not a big deal for Harmonizers to do chores for other people. They will often sacrifice time and energy for the sake of others they care about. At their best, Harmonizers can make a difference by doing things selflessly for others.

> *This year on Super Bowl Sunday, I had plans to go to my friend's house for a party. Another friend of mine threw out his back and needed to go to the hospital because he couldn't walk. I offered to take him. This friend often complains that no one is ever "on his side." By me volunteering to help him out, it re-instilled his faith in people.* (ESFJ)

> *This past summer my boyfriend's family suffered the loss of a family member. He had driven from Michigan to the east side of Ohio to visit me for a weekend. Within a few hours of arriving he received the phone call about his older cousin. He left Ohio the next morning telling me he was OK and I didn't have to come with him. I could tell he wasn't OK and decided to drive up myself to be with him and his family in their time of need. I could tell I had made a difference for the entire family by being there and running errands to make the trying time a bit easier.* (ESFJ)

> *When my boyfriend was injured at work and lost everything, I offered to help him out to relieve some stress. When my mom had surgery, I took care of her for two months after until she was able to do so on her own. I have set a strong, stable life for my three-year-old son, even though I am a single parent, and have struggled to be able to achieve that. My friend Danielle had four wisdom teeth pulled and she had no one to take care of her after until her parents got into town, so I volunteered to be there for her.* (ESFJ)

COMPARING HARMONIZERS (SFs) TO OTHER CORE PERSONALITY TYPES

Not only are Harmonizers not all alike, they also share some similarities with other core personality types. Generally characterized as making a difference by focusing on the people involved in a situation and by doing even impersonal things in a personal manner, Harmonizers (SFs) share a preference for Sensing with Stabilizers (STs—described in chapter 4). Both Harmonizers and Stabilizers are likely to pay attention to details, realities, and the present situation, though Stabilizers are more likely to focus on the situation itself in a logical and objective manner.

Harmonizers also share a preference for Feeling with Catalysts (NFs—described in chapter 6). Both Harmonizers and Catalysts may come across as being quite concerned about their values, especially the people-oriented values at work or in a relationship. Harmonizers are likely to focus on the details and the individuals of the immediate situation, while Catalysts are likely to look for patterns and interconnections among the details and seek a way to mobilize people to address the long-term causes of the situation.

Harmonizers generally have the least in common with Visionaries (NTs—described in chapter 7). They are likely to have a shorter-term focus than Visionaries and show a more practical, matter-of-fact approach to a situation and also pay more attention to a particular individual they may want to help feel included or may want to rescue.

EXERCISES FOR HARMONIZERS

Before you move on to chapter 6, complete exercises 8 and 9 to help you determine how likely you are to use the themes described in this chapter to make a difference at work and in your relationships.

Using Harmonizer (SF) Characteristics to Make a Difference at Work

Rate the extent to which you are likely to use the Harmonizer themes described in this chapter to make a difference in a work situation, on the following scale:

0 = Almost never
1 = Seldom
2 = Occasionally
3 = Frequently
4 = Almost always

1. Being there for others (care for, accept, and support others; don't judge; listen)   0 1 2 3 4

2. Being positive (be optimistic, appreciative, approachable, and enthusiastic)   0 1 2 3 4

3. Being inclusive (set a fun tone; take a playful initiative in team building; make teammates feel included)   0 1 2 3 4

4. Getting to know others personally (learn about coworkers and bosses on a personal level; provide personalized service to customers)   0 1 2 3 4

5. Being respectful, behaving properly (advocate the golden rule; demonstrate values and ethics to coworkers; promote fairness, civility, equality)   0 1 2 3 4

6. Smoothing conflict (be accommodating; avoid conflict-producing issues; make situations less stressful)   0 1 2 3 4

7. Showing loyalty to the organization (be dedicated to the organization and its people; be willing to volunteer; stay committed)   0 1 2 3 4

continues

Exercise 8 cont'd

8. Rescuing individuals (stand up for others; help   0 1 2 3 4
lost souls; cheer for the underdog; create kinder,
gentler, more fair workplace)

9. Providing comfort (be concerned with comfort,   0 1 2 3 4
accommodations, and aesthetics of workplace)

10. Creating order (instill orderliness; create a   0 1 2 3 4
clean, safe environment)

Be sure to save these ratings because you will be asked to use them in
the planning exercises in chapter 8.

EXERCISE 9

Using Harmonizer (SF) Characteristics to Make a Difference in Relationships

Rate the extent to which you are likely to use the Harmonizer themes
described in this chapter to make a difference in a *relationship* situation, on the following scale:

0 = Almost never
1 = Seldom
2 = Occasionally
3 = Frequently
4 = Almost always

1. Being there for others (care for, accept, and   0 1 2 3 4
support others; don't judge; listen)

2. Offering encouragement (offer encourage-   0 1 2 3 4
ment; get others to believe in themselves)

3. Verbalizing feelings (be open and encourage   0 1 2 3 4
others to be open; express feelings directly and
matter-of-factly, but politely)

continues

Exercise 9 cont'd

4. Being loyal (trust others; create sense of togetherness and belonging) 0 1 2 3 4

5. Making others happy (smile and get others to smile; offer affection and other acts of kindness; smooth hurt feelings; show appreciation) 0 1 2 3 4

6. Rescuing others (support lost souls and underdogs; help others get out of bad situations) 0 1 2 3 4

7. Hosting (connect people at parties and events; make others feel included and comfortable) 0 1 2 3 4

8. Smoothing conflict (play role of peacemaker; offer forgiveness; smooth ruffled feathers) 0 1 2 3 4

9. Advocating values (make decisions based on values; know right from wrong; encourage proper behavior) 0 1 2 3 4

10. Sacrificing for others (do chores for people; spend time and energy selflessly on others) 0 1 2 3 4

Be sure to save these ratings because you will be asked to use them in the planning exercises in chapter 8.

How "Catalysts" (NFs) Can Make a Difference

People with preferences for Intuition (N) and Feeling (F) tend to be good communicators who believe in championing causes for the good of others. We will refer to these NF types as "Catalysts." If you have determined by looking at the middle preferences of your four-letter MBTI type that you are a Catalyst (that is, an NF), this chapter is especially for you. You may also want to read this chapter to learn more about others who have this core personality type.

We'll start with a "scouting report" on people with this core personality type and then move to a more detailed description of these and other tendencies reported in the research studies.

Scouting Report on Catalysts

Catalysts tend to . . .
- Provide personal warmth, enthusiasm, and energy toward the discovery and development of possibilities
- Be insightful and creative
- Believe in causes, especially people-oriented causes

continues

Catalysts cont'd

- Have a gift for communicating with passion and emphasize values
- Be energized by relationships and connections
- Keep structures, roles, and procedures as flexible as possible so that people can grow naturally within them
- Exhibit high bursts of energy
- Initially see the good in all and push for their long-term development
- Value authenticity, harmony, and inspiration
- Want things to be enjoyable, meaningful, and fun

Overall, Catalysts tend to make a difference . . .

- **At work** by inspiring people to contribute their strengths to the organization they care about and to their relationships with the people working there
- **In relationships** by encouraging growth and insight and by communicating energetically

A MORE DETAILED LOOK AT CATALYSTS

Once again, be sure to keep in mind that the descriptions of Catalysts that follow reflect general tendencies only. They are not true for all people with preferences for Intuition and Feeling. Furthermore, people with any of the other three core personality types could be found to exhibit the characteristics provided in the descriptions because situations—as well as personality preferences—drive behavior. Nevertheless, in general, these descriptions will help in your understanding of this core personality type.

Catalysts bring a personal warmth and enthusiasm to the discovery and examination of possibilities. They want to understand the meaning of messages, people, and life itself. At their best they tend to be insightful, creative, and capable of charming others with their communication skills. They are believers and make decisions and try to motivate people based on the possibilities and principles of their beliefs. They are attracted to new projects that have implications for people and their development more than to concrete production projects. They are interested in the patterns that underlie facts and words and want to use their insights to explore human relationships. Their personal warmth enhances their gift for communicating and can convey both the possibilities they see and the values attached to those possibilities. Research indicates they have an interest in both providing and receiving psychological services, particularly those that emphasize a person-oriented approach. They seek environments and circles of people who are big-picture oriented, creative, and values driven.

Catalysts prefer to work in an organization that stands for something they believe in, that is innovative and future oriented, and that uses strategies that emphasize development and relationships. They want organizations to be loosely structured, with job descriptions that allow people to evolve and grow. They prefer flexible procedures that allow people to use their personal judgments and hunches. They bring energy to brainstorming sessions designed to discover alternatives.

As leaders, Catalysts are typically democratic, charismatic (maybe even dramatic), idealistic, and enthusiastic. They are typically sociable types who compliment others freely, smooth over conflicts (unless the conflict involves firmly held values), operate in high bursts of energy, and are open to possible modifications to their decisions. They initially find the good in all colleagues, though if you offend a Catalyst, you may lose his or her support. Catalysts push for the development of all members of the organization and are often staunch supporters of training and educational opportunities.

Catalysts like to use their dominant skills and encourage others to use theirs. Their communication skills often lead them into customer service or public relations. They can be empathetic and generally see people as good and important. They value innovation, stimulation, harmony, and authenticity. They sometimes get so excited about possibilities that they become overextended and are not typically known to be disciplinarians. They love both to talk and listen and judge success by the energy in the room. If you show that an idea will lead to the enhancement of relationships or provide new insights and perspectives, they are likely to support your point of view. Just make sure the process is enjoyable, meaningful, and fun.

On teams, Catalysts enjoy exercises that provide insight into what matters to people. They tend to celebrate diversity and want everyone to work together for the common cause. They may hope that someone else on the team is interested in dealing with the control functions regarding costs, schedules, and other detailed facts and figures.

For Catalysts, many of these same tendencies show up in their relationships outside work as well. In fact, all kinds of relationships (with lovers, friends, acquaintances, neighbors, associates, and so on) are very important to them. They provide warmth, insight, and enthusiasm and expect the same from others. They care about the people and causes in their lives. They are energized by relationships, whether those are personal or networking engagements.

HOW CATALYSTS (NFs) TEND TO DIFFER

Of course, not all Catalysts are alike. For example, NFs with a preference for Introversion (INFs) may be hesitant to express their feelings verbally, but their actions speak to their sympathy and caring for others and they often find fulfillment in literature or visual arts that communicate the human experience. Extroverted NFs (ENFs) are more likely to show their belief in people collectively and lead change efforts with messages germane to the values of the cause, with exhortations such as "We can do this if we work together." They are often blessed with wonderful communication skills and, at their best, may be quite charismatic. Catalysts with a preference for Judging (NFJs) may tend to come across as being more adamant. Their firm beliefs may cause them to try to convert others and avoid or disdain people who are disloyal to their cause. Those with a preference for Perceiving (NFPs) may appear more flexible and may sometimes care more about the relationship than a particular cause. Energetic and creative, they can see all points of view and be less willing to stay focused.

CATALYSTS (NFs) MAKING A DIFFERENCE AT WORK

Let's look at how Catalysts, when using the strengths of their natural preferences, can make a difference at work. Each of the following themes represents characteristics expressed by Catalyst participants from the research studies. Each theme is illustrated by stories written by the participants, with the storyteller's four-letter type provided at the end of each story.

Theme 1: Reaching Dreams

Catalysts tend to want to believe in the organization they work for and encourage the development of its growth and potential. At their best they help promote long-term development, transformational change, and a sense of being part of something bigger. Their idealism can be contagious, and they help others become what they are capable of becoming.

> *Several years ago I was asked to sit on a global women's marketing task force. Although I was expected to be just an observer, I was able to put forth the solution to a problem. The concept was very well received and worked its way up the ladder until I eventually was asked to present it in Paris to the top three executives of a huge international auto manufacturing company. The idea never made it into reality, but it got the task force on the radar big-time.* **(INFP)**

> *I worked with adults with developmental disabilities. I secured employment for them, trained them, and followed through on their successes. I arranged accommodations to ensure success as a benefit to both the employed and the employer. I always advocate for my people. I support their dreams and interests. I feel they produce more and apply themselves more fully with my support. I instill, encourage, and empower the employees I manage to share their ideas,*

*and I always follow through. I believe what matters most to
them matters to me as well. That's my philosophy outside of
work as well.*   **(ENFP)**

*About six months ago I got my first full-time real job at a
prestigious, renowned health care institute. I remember
how excited I was when I first started. I was in the department that I wanted to work in, Human Resources. I was
working for a nonprofit organization that is dedicated to
curing cancer. This all really sparked an interest in me,
and for the first time in my life I felt that I could really
be part of something great . . . something that could
really make a difference! When I began to settle in, I
started to quickly realize the politics in the office. One
of the first things I noticed was that the HR department
was extremely divided. There is an operations side and
an employment side. The director of operations and the
director of employment were both fifty-year-old women
who don't care for each other. This caused a division in
the department. I worked on the operations side and
became friends with the girls on the employment side.
We all agreed how ridiculous it all was. We began to
plan get-togethers as one department. I feel like I made
a difference in the department. I feel like I started the
process of merging the sides together. I look forward to
the "Kringle Mingle" that we planned for the week before
Christmas. It is my hope that we will continue the process
of merging as one department and work more closely with
each other.*   **(ENFP)**

Theme 2: Seeing Good in Everyone

Catalysts typically see the good in people. You can perhaps prove
you are no good to Catalysts by being disingenuous, but they tend
to prefer to focus on the good. This naturally leads them to cele-

brate diversity. They generally don't want gossip going around that separates or divides the group. If there are differences, they tend to seek a win-win solution to keep the group united and use the good ideas found in opposing points of view.

> *I am a housing property manager for a large community, responsible for about twenty employees—twelve from the maintenance department team. One of these men, we'll call him "Rob," was extremely talented. He could fix ANYTHING. Rob definitely would have been the next supervisor but he had two problems he could not control: he drank too much and smoked the "wacky tobacco" every day. I had several talks with Rob about his weaknesses, but he did not really think he had a problem. One time he showed up at a resident's home after having several drinks. It could have been an immediate dismissal from our company, but Rob was written up with a warning this time. It happened again the following month—again I had to write him up, but I avoided any further discipline.*
>
> *Finally, Rob was sweating a pipe one morning and he caught a piece of insulation on fire. The devastating result was that six entire apartments were burnt. This was Rob's last chance; I terminated him that day. I felt I had to. He was very upset and begged for forgiveness. This event took place almost two years ago now. Rob and I still keep in touch. Every time I talk to him, he thanks me for terminating his employment and wishes that I had done it sooner. When I ask him why, he says, "You gave me a wakeup call." He now attends AA meetings and another support group, states that his marriage is 110 percent better, and now has a more financially satisfying career as a maintenance supervisor. I always tell him that he gives me too much credit; it was he who made the change, but if I gave him the extra little push by terminating his employment, I am glad that it all worked out for him.* **(ENFP)**

When I worked in a law firm as a clerk, I didn't like that there was always a lot of office gossip going on because I saw it as detrimental to the amount and quality of work that could be done. Plus it threatened good relationships between coworkers and led to a lack of trust between coworkers. As a young employee at my first "office" job, I was eager to learn and be productive, so I refrained from passing on information and even refused to listen to such conversations. In this manner, I gained respect and trust from my coworkers because they saw me as a serious and dedicated employee. A few smart people in the firm caught on to my professional behavior. They asked me why I was so serious. I would justify my actions as being responsible and professional. They agreed that I had a point and so they cut out their gossiping mainly to gain trust and respect.   **(INFP)**

At the bar I worked at, not everybody got along, and there was a lot of drama when I started working there. I tend to be very friendly and want everyone to get along. I became friends with everyone despite what people would say about each other. Pretty soon the manager noticed how I got along with my coworkers, and I was commended for coming in with an open mind and becoming friends quickly with everyone. I kind of liked the drama but I kept it interesting without it being disruptive.   **(ENFJ)**

Theme 3: Facilitating Communication

At their best, Catalysts are generally blessed with good communication skills, and thus can make a difference for organizations through public relations, marketing, and image making. Their gifts in language may also mean that they can serve others through translating—whether from language to language or from corporate speak to plain English.

At the computer store where I worked, a deaf man approached my counter. He signaled me for a pen. We ended up writing back and forth on Post-it notes and having a complete conversation with written words. As my counter became busy, I paged another employee to help out while I kept helping my deaf customer. Eventually I was able to give him the product he needed, as well as a plethora of other information. He shook my hand and thanked me for being so patient with him. **(INFP)**

In the army I was a gunner on the mortar squad. Once when I was stationed in Germany, our company was convoying on civilian streets when we were stopped by some German construction workers. They did not speak English, and my commander did not speak German. Some guys knew I spoke German, and word spread back along the convoy that I was needed. I helped translate and solve the communication problem. I have been told that I make a difference with my communication skills. That sure helped that day. The convoy moved on. **(ENFP)**

I worked at a big high-end retail store in a mall for three years. A way that I learned to make a difference in customer service was through my positive attitude. With our stringent return policy we often had customers who weren't willing to accept it. Customers would come back with worn jeans and ready to argue for a return. I never raised my voice, acted agitated, or was unpleasant. I often just smiled and said, "Sorry, but no." This led to my feeling better and the customers feeling better, and coworkers found a new way to deal with difficult customers. One day a young man came in to return a denim outfit he said he hadn't worn. It looked like someone had rolled around in the dirt with it on. I apologized and was nice and calmly explained to him we couldn't take it back. I told him, "I believe you haven't worn

the outfit, but someone did. You need to find that person so
he can pay you for the outfit. It wasn't very nice for your
friend to do that." He had nothing to come back with. He
started out very angry and then eventually was nicer and
left. Soon after my peers had heard what happened, they
thought it was a great way of dealing with problem cus-
tomers. A few of them even started doing it, too.   **(ENFP)**

There was a supervisor at my work who talked down to
people and disrespectfully in other ways, too. Colleagues
were afraid to confront this. I raised the matter with the
next level of management without naming names. But
the disrespectful supervisor joined the conversation and
claimed that there was no such thing as a good tone vs. a
bad tone. As she said this, she proved herself guilty by the
way she spoke to me disrespectfully. Later the manager and
my peers thanked me for speaking up, and eventually the
disrespectful supervisor was coached to change her tone
toward employees. I believe that it is not just what you say
but how you say it.   **(INFJ)**

Theme 4: Rescuing Groups of People

Catalysts tend to believe in causes and are ready advocates for
such causes. They may go beyond rescuing individuals to rallying
people to stand up for the rights of whole groups of people. They
have been known to advocate for customers and employees alike.

At one point I did billing and prior authorization for a den-
tal clinic that serviced physically/mentally challenged folks
as well as those with cancer or AIDS and those requiring
transplants. Many of our patients were under- or uninsured,
and often their bills were very high. On numerous occasions
I was able to obtain a lead for the patient in the direction
of supplemental insurance. I also did lots of investigation to

see if their treatment could be billed as medical, therefore relieving much stress about their bills since they obviously had more pressing medical issues to deal with.   **(INFP)**

I decided to bring up to my boss that we should receive a pay increase in our salary for job longevity. We get a base salary plus commission. They only established this pay structure a year ago. I had my two-year review recently and brought up the idea and was given a salary pay increase in addition to my commission. I feel like I was the one to make a difference in everyone's pay, not just my own. I am glad I spoke up and presented the idea to my boss. Just recently another coworker also received a pay increase as well. I made a difference in his life and feel great about it. **(ENFJ)**

I make a difference at work by simply getting involved. I am a team leader, a health and safety rep, and a quality rep. If there is any way to improve the organization and the quality of the work lives of my coworkers, I like to be an advocate and get involved. It is very important to me to improve con stantly. For example, as a health and safety rep for my area, I designed an action plan to promote the use of earplugs. In a factory setting, it is very loud day in and day out, and it is hazardous to work without earplugs. I first set up appointments for everybody to get their hearing tested. I motivated them by offering a free coffee or Dairy Queen if they did so. I would then go around every day before everyone would start working and pass out earplugs, encouraging their use. This went on for several months, and people were very receptive. Many people realized that when they were not wearing earplugs, it could not be good for their long-term hearing.   **(ENFJ)**

I learned about how to set up an emergency operating center (EOC) in my public administration master's degree

*program. When visiting Lebanon, the war broke out but
not near my small city. Refugees poured into the city, and
I talked to the mayor about what I had learned in my program and then helped establish a plan for an EOC in the
city. I was put in charge of the incidents command post that
distributed food and clean water to the refugees. So I ended
up making a big difference by applying what I learned in
my class in the U.S. in a situation halfway around the world.*

(INFJ)

Theme 5: Developing People's Potential

NFs often serve as agents for change at the individual as well as
group/organization level. Many Catalysts strongly value personal
growth and may make a difference by teaching or facilitating the
learning of life's lessons. They generally want to help develop
potential—not just technical skills. They tend to want to see people
develop their knowledge and skills to become all they can be.

*For two consecutive summers, I recruited, facilitated, and
oversaw a mentor program for minority female teenagers.
I dedicated my time and energy to help these ladies understand their worth, potential, and greatness. I prepared many
seminars and lessons on little things that make a big difference, such as their character, attitudes, and perception. The
lessons focused on leadership, virtue, and purpose. I got
them to think of short- and long-term goals and the importance of education. For many of the ladies, being a part of
my summer mentor program kept them out of trouble. They
gained positive friendships with each other and formed
a support system among themselves. Not only did this
impact on positive changes with the teen ladies, but it also
helped me. I learned my strengths and weaknesses. I also
learned what my passion in life is. I learned that I am very*

fulfilled when I'm helping people, mentoring them, or giving. I have a passion for teens and teaching them through words and actions.   **(INFP)**

I worked at an advertising agency that had lots of people outside the creative department (like accountants, media, research, account planning types, etc.) who were suddenly being asked to come up with new ideas to advance their own areas of expertise, and they couldn't do it. They had no experience with how to think creatively. So I looked for ways to solve this problem and found a technique that would help. I talked the company into paying for my certification in this technique. I came back and taught it to about five hundred staffers. It created a huge buzz. It is now in general use in most important meetings throughout the agency and is largely responsible for creating a large-scale "culture change" and helping to move the agency closer to its vision of generating "Never Before Thinking." Three years later it is still in use.   **(INFP)**

I worked with new production supervisors to get them ready to present information to top management about their plant operations. I gained regular feedback about how I have increased skill level and confidence. They told me how the skills that I taught them will be with them forever. An individual from China told me that when he speaks to others he hears my voice saying "slow down." In a past job, I served as an outplacement consultant and helped hundreds of people learn the skills to gain new jobs and careers. This involved teaching résumé writing, interviewing skills, marketing, and other topics. When a local brewery closed, my work helped 98 percent of the individuals find new jobs within one year.   **(ENFJ)**

Theme 6: Developing Belief/Value Systems

Catalysts tend to personalize the mission of the organization. They often want to work in a setting and for an organization that stands for the values they believe in. While they may celebrate the profitability of the company, they will still want to make sure that success benefits the people, too. They might make a difference in an organization by attempting to use the values of its vision statement strategically.

> *I was a manager at a pool where at the end of every summer the pool would turn green. No one could figure it out. I researched the possibilities and found the reason. I forwarded this information to my boss and also created a "managers book" in light of a lot of confusion that comes with the tasks and duties of opening, running, and managing the pool. My book entailed in specific detail the ins and outs of all tasks and goals of our pool. It now gets used every summer for new managers and has helped decrease costs, eliminate the green pool problem, and help to more efficiently run the operations. I was a varsity swimmer in high school in this community and I am glad to make a difference by ensuring that there will be a quality place to swim and learn swimming.* **(ENFP)**

> *I am on a "Quality Team" at work. We meet weekly and discuss issues and come up with plans to fix them. Changes are made in the current procedure to make the system move efficiently and with a balance for employee satisfaction. We (as employees) have a very structured position. We receive charges due to any errors, and our process currently has the charges passed out randomly. This has decreased morale, which in turn causes frustration, which increases the likelihood of making more errors and with no visible record for the employee. It is hard to target specific problems and give the needed training. I proposed a two-part and partial*

solution. I suggested we create a spreadsheet to serve as a recording device. That eliminates the random passing of charges and recording when the error occurred and thus we (as employees) can check the charges by a deadline. This created accountability for employees and minimized the decrease in morale, created a control mechanism for staff, and reduced time searching for employees and passing out and picking up.   (ENFJ)

I like to volunteer. I went to a private school growing up and often participated in volunteering work because we had to for service hours. But just because we had to doesn't mean I didn't enjoy it. I loved it. So last year I decided to volunteer at the local health clinic. I go once a week and do simple jobs like label birth control, file and organize, talk with people, and help out the ladies in the office with their jobs. I always go there with my roommate, and we always have fun. The ladies that work there love our help and beg us to come all the time. Not only do they enjoy our help but they enjoy our company. It's a great organization that helps women and men all over. I am pleased to be a part of an organization that helps people of all ages solve personal life issues.   (ENFP)

Theme 7: Promoting Change Through Relationships

Catalysts can often help motivate others to change for the sake of big-picture goals, standards, and values. For example, they may seek to facilitate relationships between units and departments. They generally strive for unity and promote the notion that "we're all in this together."

I was working as a manager of a fast-food restaurant, and it was coming up to the end of the year when the store manager needed to do reviews of the employees. The store manager hated reviews because they were long and complicated and most times led to one of our employees getting their feelings hurt and blaming him. So I drew up a draft of a way to get the employees involved with the process. The store manager liked the idea, and we put it in place. First we explained the process to the manager. It goes like this: All employees will first grade themselves and set three goals for themselves to accomplish before the next review. Next, all the managers get together off-site to review the employees' goals and performance. Then as a team, we managers come up with a rating for each employee. Finally, the store manager sits down with employees individually to give them their review. This process was very well received by all staff members. The crew felt it was fairer. The managers felt like they had a voice in the store. Then the store manager felt that there was a lot less pressure on him.   **(ENFP)**

I am in the process of rebuilding the credibility of our work unit. Traditionally, we had bad managers in our department who seemed to work reactively, and our unit was always seen as the "processors." I am attempting to promote a greater proactive and strategic management approach. I believe in the value of HR as a true business partner that addresses people issues and organizational needs.   **(INFP)**

As a young female design student, I have often found that I need to prove myself to my male coworkers. I worked at a large home improvement store as a kitchen designer to get some hands-on experience in my field. After seeing several situations where mismeasurements required us to either reorder cabinets or "eat" the cost of a complete correction, I devised a plan to eliminate these problems in the future: double-checking each other's work (in a manner that would not offend anyone). When a client came in for a design consultation, free designers would sit quietly in the background and jot notes regarding that particular design—for example, how space would be used both functionally and aesthet-

*ically, and if there was ample room for appliances and cabi-
nets to open and close freely. No verbal criticism or suggestions would be made in front of customers. As the most
junior designer (and a female), I knew from the start that it
would be difficult to propose a plan that would be acceptable
to my coworkers. So I quickly realized I needed to propose
this plan through someone who my team respected. With the
help of my more senior "voice," we proposed this plan for
training new designers. So by our making these older designers feel as though they were ultimately training me, they felt
that they were doing an added service for our store. We
noticed that we could eliminate minor mistakes and thus
decrease loss due to costly design and measuring mistakes
without causing hard feelings among the valued designers.
I learned a valuable lesson: Not everyone needs to know
who develops a plan, and it is often a wise choice to let
someone propose a solution who has seniority to back the
idea.* **(ENFP)**

Theme 8: Being Creative

Catalysts have been known to encourage creativity and innovation
in many different ways. Many Catalysts have a discerning sense of
aesthetics for their workplace. Their creativity is often stimulated
in brainstorming sessions. They can often help others see new
ways of dealing with issues, new ways of stating a message, and
new ways of making the organization successful.

*While working at a large advertising agency, I was assigned
as a copywriter to work on a little-noticed portion of the
business. Seeing ways that this business could augment the
larger corporate image, I rewrote the strategy and wrote a
series of ten to twelve new ads that were very different from
past executions. Not only did they run as full-page ads in* USA
Today, *but the client also had them displayed alongside the*

product in their corporate exhibition hall. One of the head-
lines was made into a T-shirt and passed out at sporting
events by an enthused reader. In addition, we also received
unsolicited letters from the public telling us how inspira-
tional the messages were. All in all, it helped grow this
account into a significant piece of business. **(INFP)**

I currently work at a bookstore on campus in the textbook
department. Recently, one of our clothing/merchandise repre-
sentatives was in the store meeting with my boss. They then
called myself and a coworker of mine into their meeting and
began asking for our input on several items they were contem-
plating purchasing to sell to customers. After looking at exam-
ples and different styles of clothing, my coworker and I chose
the outfits, and that is what they decided to order and be sold.
Shortly after that my boss approached me and asked if I and
my coworker would be interested in kind of being in charge of
what merchandise would be displayed on the store's Web site,
since it is currently rather plain and boring. My boss not only
let us help him make a decision but is also giving us an oppor-
tunity to help boost the store's image by working together—
and hopefully making a positive difference. **(ENFP)**

When rearranging the floor space at work, I try to give my
advice on best traffic flow and what is visually pleasing.
One manager agreed with me and told another who
responded, "She always has good ideas." **(INFP)**

In the many different jobs that I've had there have been
many instances that have been small but may have had an
impact. When working at the Disney store, we had a lot of
plush toy merchandise, and sometimes it does not sell as
much as other merchandise. Our store's sales were low, and
we needed to meet a goal on the Finding Nemo plush toys.
So my manager asked me to create a display in the front of

the store to attract people to the Finding Nemo plush toy. I took the plush toy and rearranged it on one of our display tables, and we nearly sold out of that toy on the same day. People could not see the merchandise in its original place, and it was not grabbing anyone's attention. (INFP)

Theme 9: Providing Inspirational Motivation

Catalysts at their best tend to be enthusiastic, fun, and passionate. They often can inspire people to believe they can do difficult tasks and enjoy the journey getting there. They can be charismatic leaders, motivating people to unite and deliver for the cause.

When I worked for the bank, there was conflict among the tellers. They were all females with equally dominating personalities. I was interning as the manager of that particular banking center and was responsible for handling matters of that sort. The head teller was late coming in to work, and she's responsible for replenishing money when the other tellers run out. Well, because she wasn't there, another teller took the initiative to open the vault and get the money. When the head teller came in, she was furious that someone was in her cash vault. They had a big confrontation, which I had to handle. I sat down with them both and had them explain what the problem was. I acted as a mediator until we got to the root of the problem. After they both apologized to one another, I addressed the whole line of tellers and addressed the importance of everybody getting along and acting as a team. I explained how division messes up the team as a whole. From this conversation, I believe that the line of tellers got the picture, and for the rest of the duration that I was there, not many arguments/confrontations took place. Everyone tried to work as a team and get along. The only disagreements remaining were handled as positive conflict that resulted in greater productivity. (INFP)

*At a past job I was leading a team to accomplish their indi-
vidual sales goals. Their goals were high, but their confidence
levels were low. One day I asked them to walk around the
store with me before their shift. I picked out key sales items
and I asked them to give me as much product knowledge on
the key items as they could. They were able to give me a
great deal of information on the products and I added to
their knowledge. This took approximately fifteen minutes to
do, and at the end of it I told them that they were able to sell
those items to me, so use that tactic to sell the products to
customers. That night each associate made their sales goals
and were way above the store goal for the day. A change in
attitude and a boost of confidence never hurts.* **(ENFJ)**

*I was often left in charge of my team even though I was not
the manager. I was the one who would volunteer to help
out others and get things done. The team would have sunk
without me. I also act as the team's "cheerleader," helping
encourage my teammates and get them through difficult
times. I keep people motivated and positive by praising
them for what a good job they have done and what goals
we are accomplishing.* **(INFJ)**

Theme 10: Helping People Understand

Catalysts tend to seek and/or provide insight. They generally want
others to understand the importance of what they are doing and
how it will enhance the organization and individuals' growth and
development. They tend to want to answer all questions so people
gain meaning, not just answers.

*I am a registered respiratory therapist and love to stay on
the cutting edge of knowledge in my field. For example, I
helped a patient and his family understand the disease and
reasons for certain tests and took the time to answer all their*

questions. They told me it made a difference. I do this often. I believe it is important to be educated and knowledgeable about your illness and I encourage people to ask questions. If I don't know the answer, I find it out from someone who does. Another time I spent a lot of time with a patient who was considered a high-risk candidate for surgery. I encouraged him to ask the doctors' questions, which he was reluctant to do. I researched information for him and gave him resources to follow. When he recovered, he shared information with me and thanked me for encouraging him to ask questions.

(ENFJ)

This past summer I worked at a car dealership back home. I was a receptionist and performed such duties as answering the telephone, filing, accounting, dealing with customer problems, and other miscellaneous jobs. One of my duties I feel helped the business the most was the research I did to ensure that our accounting system worked right. Doing accounting at this dealership was a very difficult and tedious job, but it was very important, worthwhile, and pre- vented many short-term and long-term problems. My job in the accounting department was to make sure that the parts and service accounts matched. We would order parts to use in our service department. If either account was off, several things could happen to different people. These mishaps could include mechanics not being paid properly for their labor hours, inventory discrepancies (ordering too much or too little), cash not balancing correctly, and customers not getting their rebate warranty checks. I was mainly in charge of getting the accounting work done, but I still had to work with others. The service manager, parts manager, and office manager played a part in my work being able to be com- pleted. Not only did we have to discuss problems but initially we had to gather information to be able to begin the process every day. Each member of the group developed trust in the

*others that their ideas and troubleshooting techniques
would be successful. Everyone in the group made me feel
valued and appreciated for pulling everything together to
make the accounting department run smoothly.*   **(ENFJ)**

*At work we were missing information for the many different
investment products we offer. The problem we were having
is that our senior marketing staff (myself included) kept
getting caught flat-footed when we were faced with an
in-depth question about a new product line. My manager
came to just a couple of us senior marketers to try to get all
the appropriate information to any question our marketers
might face. Three of us spent nearly a week compiling information to make a "Product Bible" for the rest of the staff. It
really made me proud and happy to help out my company
and fellow employees.*   **(ENFJ)**

CATALYSTS (NFs) MAKING A DIFFERENCE IN RELATIONSHIPS

Now let's look at how Catalysts, when using the strengths of their
natural preferences, can make a difference in their personal
relationships.

Theme 1: Being Deeply Emotional

Catalysts tend to care deeply about others and freely show their emotions. They generally want to bond with people in relationships—
not merely be acquaintances. Their depth of feeling may heighten
the drama and importance of situations in their relationships.

*Six years ago my sister was working for a drug rehabilita-
tion center. She was a college student and worked part-time
caring for the children of people who were in rehab. I was a
nanny and a student as well. One day she called me saying*

that someone had left a baby girl at the center. The baby was about six months old, and her mother was in jail on possession charges. The baby's mother was not expected to return for quite some time. The center hired my sister to care for the baby twenty-four hours a day. As I sit here and type I am still amazed at the work and strength it took from all of us. My sister and I, along with my mother, took care of the baby around the clock. Since my sister was in college, we helped her by caring for the baby when she was in class and when she needed a break.

The baby was returned to her mother six months later. I have remained in constant contact with the baby and her family for the past seven years. For part of that time the baby came to live with me because the mother couldn't take care of her. It has been the most rewarding experience of my entire life. This mother doesn't know how to care for herself or for the child. I have tried to teach her how to take care of her baby and figured out how to do what is best for the baby. Most importantly, I have made a difference in the life of that one single little girl. She is amazing. To come through all of the trials and tribulations and still be happy and brilliant is something I find hard to describe. All of the things I do at work as a nanny I have done with her. I have taught her how to love and how to be loved unconditionally. I think that is life's biggest lesson. I make sure she has clothes and food and that she has toys to play with and books to read. I also make sure she has respect and, most importantly, love. She has her own room at my house with her own things. She knows she is safe and cared about at all times.   **(ENFJ)**

I skipped work and class to ride with three other friends as we drove a coworker home (three hours). Her father had died of cancer at 5 a.m., and we needed to support her on the trip home. She actually was told that he was "real bad"

*and to hurry home to say good-bye. It turned out that we
didn't make it in time. We sat with Jennifer and let her talk
about whatever was on her mind. The four of us became
very close and would gather regularly and play "You've Got a
Friend"—demonstrating/declaring our commitment and
friendship to each other. I am still in touch with them seven
years later.*

(ENFP)

Theme 2: Advocating for Causes

Catalysts are likely to advocate for causes outside of work as well
as within. At their best they tend to want to help produce a better
world. They may be willing to dedicate their time and resources to
rescue their community.

*After several robberies occurred in my neighborhood, I
helped to organize a block watch program for the community where I live. Two neighbors and I organized neighborhood meetings to help stop the violence and robberies.
Within two weeks the robberies had decreased and the
neighborhood was safer (even though the families in the
area took turns staying awake to patrol the area).* (INFP)

*It started when my staff had me "arrested" for the American
Cancer Society's "jail and bail" fund-raising event a couple
of years ago. I had absolutely no idea that this was going
to happen, so I was not prepared for it (I didn't have phone
numbers of people to call and so on). The purpose was to
call anyone and everyone in order to "raise your bail and
get out of jail." All of the collected money would be used
right here in our county for research, education, and patient
services. My bail was set at $250. They gave me a telephone
and phone book, and I got busy. I called everyone that I
knew in my personal and professional lives and soon not*

only made my bail but had a grand total of $1,405. They thanked me, took my picture, and gave me the mug and "mug shot." It was a great feeling to have contributed to such a good local cause. Before they brought me back to work (in a police car!), I was asked to be on their "MOST WANTED" poster for the next year's campaign. This was an honor. By being one of the MOST WANTED, I had to commit to raise a minimum of $2,000. I exceeded my goal and plan to participate in this philanthropy next year, too!

(ENFP)

My dad has always had strong political and environmental beliefs. He knew he wanted to speak out in some way, so he and I decided to protest with a small group from my hometown. We got our word out, and even after I moved away he continues to be a part of this group. He has gotten my mom and brother involved, along with coworkers. The group not only protests but does community dinners for the needy every Sunday. It's an excellent organization that I enjoyed being a part of while I was around.   (ENFJ)

Theme 3: Creating Fun

Catalysts often have a gift for developing creative plans for fun and surprises. Their creative juices tend to produce spontaneous fun, too. Catalysts can make a difference in relationships by making life enjoyable for all.

I have been dating Ricky for two years now. Funny thing is, for the past twelve months I only see him on Saturdays and Sundays (more on vacations). He is an engineer and has spent the past year building a car line in Mississippi. Not the greatest job for a fun-loving twenty-three-year-old with all his friends and family in Michigan missing him. It has been real hard. To make it better for him, I send him care packages of photos and my mom's banana nut bread. We have taken numerous vacations with his frequent flyer miles, and I do all the planning. I make my weekends available for him and get all of our friends together so he can have fun while he's here. We make sure we talk to each other at least once a day. If he didn't have me, it would probably be harder for him. Of course if I didn't have him, I would be sad. Even missing him all the time is better than being without him. The GREATEST thing I ever did for him was last year I planned a surprise birthday party for him. He wasn't very excited about his birthday. He felt "old" turning twenty-three. It was his first fall out of college, his new job was difficult, most of his friends were out of state or unavailable—he was a walking frown. The whole day of his birthday he couldn't get ahold of any of his friends. He was all pouty. So I suggested we go to Tony's and see if she would want to go out. Ricky reluctantly went with me, pouting, until he opened Tony's door and ALL of his friends were there. He glowed all night. I felt great for it. **(ENFP)**

I enjoy surprising people. I planned and executed a surprise birthday party for my mom's fiftieth birthday. I really got into sending out invites, making food and goodies, and getting a friend of hers to take her away for two hours while I set up and got everyone in the house. She was taken by surprise and loved that I would go out of my way to bring all of her old high school friends over. **(ENFP)**

Theme 4: Helping Others with Their Relationships

Catalysts tend to be interested in relationships—their own and those of others. They often have a knack for facilitating groups and counseling others. They want insights to be gained from their own relationships and see this as a major avenue for personal growth.

> *I am a very good listener and am great at offering advice on relationships. For example, one of our friends has a daughter with his on-and-off girlfriend. They do not live together, and the daughter (three years old) stays with her mom. Whenever our friend went to pick up his daughter, she would not want to leave her mom, and he would end up spending the day with his girlfriend and her family. I told him that he has to start having her bring his daughter to his house and dropping her off. They tried this, and he said it was working great. When he can spend the day with just his daughter, he is able to think more clearly about their situation. I have helped other friends and family with issues in their lives. I can sometimes be helpful in creating the right words to say to help people get their message across in a diplomatic way so they command respect without attacking the other party.* (INFJ)

> *I was married in my early twenties to a man whose father was a four-star general. Although successful in his professional career, he was not successful in nurturing his relationship with his son. I believe a lot of what went wrong in our relationship was a result of their relationship. My husband longed to be close to his father. He could remember an exact date, location, and time that his father played catch with him. As our relationship deteriorated, I spoke with his father and explained how his son felt. This initiated a family meeting where my ex-husband and his dad left the room to a private space and talked for hours. My ex told his dad about all his pent-up feelings and even cried. I am pretty sure his father did also. This brought them together and helped their relationship. Although we ended*

up in divorce, my ex was glad to begin rebuilding a rela-
tionship with his dad. **(ENFJ)**

I have given friends advice about what they should do in
their relationships when asked; when there is something
that is bugging me I talk to the person about it. For exam-
ple, I have a friend whose boyfriend I do not care for. I try
to tell her all the reasons she should not be with him, but if
she decides to stay with him, I will support her. **(INFP)**

Theme 5: Encouraging Others to Take Risks

Catalysts can often get others to follow their heart's desires. They
have been known to boost people's confidence to take the risks
necessary to explore beyond their current life circumstances. They
naturally understand that change is rarely possible without significant risk taking. They often help those they care about summon
the courage to try.

I am in a fraternity that has a lot of focus on ethical leader-
ship development. A few years back, we had a new member
who joined to open a new door to social activities. The new
member was very friendly, and the more I got to know him,
the more I realized he had a heart of gold and was brilliant.
His only problem was that he was unbelievably shy and
very uncomfortable in social situations because of a stutter.
Being not only a very popular member in my fraternity and
Greek life but also well connected on campus, I took him
under my wing and began introducing him to many differ-
ent kinds of people. His confidence began building as I
pointed out (truthfully) how much everyone liked him and
his company. I encouraged him to run for VP of our fraternity
(which he did and won). At this point, he was springboarded
into many leadership positions on campus. He is currently
VP of the fraternity and VP of the collegiate interfraternity
council, and is quite the hit with several sororities. He has

*thanked me many times for helping him grow socially and
as a leader.*   (ENFJ)

*I can recall a time when a friend of mine was having trouble
with school. She was wondering if she should continue her
education or follow her heart's desire. I explained to her
that following after her heart's desire would give her the
most pleasure. I hope the feedback that I gave her will be
something she can use for the rest of her life.*   (INFP)

*Back when I was a high school English teacher, I often ran
into kids who didn't know where they were headed. One
year, on a snow day, I used the time off to work on a quilt I
had been making. Mid-morning, I answered a knock on my
door only to find that it was one of my students . . . a personable kid with average grades. He wasn't a real standout
except sometimes as class clown. He was a senior and not
sure what to do with his life. He came in and sat down. He
talked, and I sewed. He talked some more, and I played it
back for him. He ended up talking for about five hours as I
sewed. When he finally left, he had it all figured out. I don't
actually remember what he decided to do. I just remember
listening, nodding my head a lot, and sometimes repeating
what he just said. I'm glad he figured it out because I am
not sure I would have. Anyway, when he left, he hugged me
(pretty unusual for a student, considering it was 1969) and
thanked me for spending so much time helping him "get
his head together." Then he got on his motorcycle and rode
away. I never saw him again. I guess I'll never know how his
life turned out. But I have a feeling that if he hadn't figured
it out, he would have showed up at my door another day.*
                                                    (INFP)

Theme 6: Being Inspirational

Catalysts generally prefer to make decisions in their lives in accordance with their beliefs. This is seen by many as an admirable

trait. They may express their beliefs in an inspirational manner and may sometimes advocate the conversion of beliefs of their friends and family members. They may be charismatic both at work and outside work.

I think the biggest difference I've ever made in someone's life is when I convinced my niece to enroll in college. She had graduated from high school and did not go to college right away. I had reenrolled at a local college after having my daughter but I talked her into going to MSU because I really wanted the best for her. She is three years younger than I am, so we are more like sisters. I gave her all kinds of info and even told her who to talk to in order to get in quickly. I took her to the administration building and helped her get her paperwork in. She ended up graduating two years ago and even graduated before me. **(INFP)**

I am a recovering alcoholic. I attend AA meetings regularly. Two weeks ago I was asked to speak at a large area meeting with about three hundred in attendance. I spoke, sharing my "experience, strength, and hope" with the newcomers. After the meeting, many unfamiliar faces came up, emotional, and thanked me for my story. I hope that my experience has helped some of them continue attending meetings and recover from the disease of alcoholism. I also sponsor several young (and old) men in the program. I help guide them through the twelve steps and explain the program of AA to them. I also serve as an ear that they can be completely honest with. This helps them, I think, but more importantly, listening to them helps me to forget my own troubles and get out of my head. **(ENFP)**

My mom and dad had ten children together, me being number eight. Because we have a big family, it is imperative that we are organized, structured, and together. Knowing this, I decided to hold a family meeting once a month to discuss holidays, birthdays, events, and so on to make everyone feel loved. I also held once-a-month prayers and led motivational discussions in regards to our dreams, aspirations, and goals in our lives. The meetings became very emotional, where we all expressed ourselves, our concerns for the family, and our love for one another. I then initiated a three-week fast in order for us to get on the same page, focus, and do better for ourselves. I sent out a letter to each of my siblings and parents to get on the right paths. As a result of these frequent get-togethers my family has become a lot closer and dedicated to God and more in tune with what God wants to do in each of our lives. Since then my mom has answered her call to the ministry as a pastor, and my siblings are much closer to God. The time, effort, and investments put into these meetings were definitely worth it.   **(INFP)**

Theme 7: Using Communication Skills

Catalysts are often blessed with a creative use of language. They are often willing to get the word out to people they care about. They make use of analogies and metaphors in interpersonal communications, not just when they are in front of a crowd.

My son wanted to transfer from a state university to a more expensive, out-of-state art school. His father was dead set against it. I was able to help my son find a new way to articulate his wishes to his father (I gave him a few reasons his dad could believe in). He has since been two years at this new school and receiving the best grades of his life. He is now very happily pursuing his new major as a photographer. He later sent me a note thanking me for "basically getting him in to his new school."   **(INFP)**

I'm in an investment club that is now five years old. Some members were leaving because they were too busy and couldn't maintain the responsibilities to the club to the level they thought was expected. As the VP, I suggested to the president that we have an open discussion about what was happening and how we could retain their interest and motivation as our club's focus changed from learning the basics to managing a portfolio of stocks. I led this process and sent out some questions to everyone ahead of time with an agenda for this special meeting. While facilitating the discussion we learned that several people had considered leaving and were looking for ways to make the meetings less structured and more fun. I gingerly had to reflect what I was hearing from different segments of the group. Some are family members, very conservative; others are younger professionals seeking to make the club meetings more social in nature. As a result of the process, we created a new standard agenda with open forum time to catch up for small group (committee) meetings to occur. The energy and motivation among our members has increased. Members feel more comfortable expressing ideas. We even were able to bring one member back. **(ENFP)**

Theme 8: Growing in Relationships

For some Catalysts, relationships represent the meaning of life. They may push others to explore the long-term implications and/or impact of relationships. They may help people assess whether a relationship is worth the effort on the basis of whether it is helping each person grow.

I try to make a difference in relationships every day. Dad has centered his life on his immediate family and does all he can to support us. I have tried to do/say things to make him proud of me/himself . . . this is what makes him happy. Mom has been hit hard with an empty nest and menopause. I try to talk to her as much as possible and remind her of how much she has done for me and is still doing for me. I recently made her a compilation of songs she can listen to while she exercises. They are songs we both enjoy. My two brothers and I have had a tendency to compete on all levels. I try to make sure we maintain healthy relationships and use our competition in a positive way. I try to let them know how much I learn from them. I keep in contact with many friends and have both strong and weak ties among them. Along with my family, they are my passion in life. Anything I can do to foster a positive relationship comes naturally to me.   (ENFP)

I met my best friend—in my heart, my sister—over ten years ago through a mutual friend, and we hit it off right away. During the time that we have been friends, we have become close to each other's families. My family and I realized that her parents didn't do anything for her birthdays or Christmas. They mostly concerned themselves with her younger siblings. So my parents and I have always made sure that her birthday and Christmas are very special and that she receives plenty of gifts and good thoughts. When her daughter was born in 1999, we included her in this tradition, and now every year they spend the holidays with us. By these actions we were able to give her back the joy of her birthday and of Christmas and carried that tradition on to her daughter so that they both have great holidays. This has bonded us as best friends and sisters, as now she is a part of my family and we all view her that way. I think that we made a difference in her life and her daughter's by changing the way she was treated.   (ENFP)

Chris and I have been best friends for sixteen years. We are as close as sisters and can almost read each other's mind. Chris is two years younger than I am. I feel that I am her role model. I feel that I have made a big difference in her all-around life. She has a pretty hard life. I always tell her everything is going to be all right. When she is excited about something I get excited for her and support her decisions. We have developed a trust that will be there forever. We introduce each other to new and exciting things while still keeping our own identity. We accept and respect each other's differences, likes, and dislikes. When one of us has a problem with work, parents, or guys, we discuss the possible options and work it out. Both of us have big dreams and goals. We motivate and encourage each other to accomplish them. In some situations we don't see eye to eye. Compromising is something we do well to sort out our differences. I show her every day that I care with encouragement and support. She knows that I will always be there for her any time of the day or night no matter what the situation is. Once in a while we get into a fight. When that occurs we sit down and share our feelings and discuss why we are upset with the other instead of screaming and yelling. We enjoy being together and share many of the same ideas, values, interests, and characteristics. This is a friendship that I hope lasts forever.   (ENFJ)

Theme 9: Showing Empathy, Not Just Sympathy

Catalysts tend to want to experience a depth of feeling in relationships. They want to understand the people they relate to—what it would be like to walk in their shoes. They naturally tend to honor the will of others without having to agree with them. They encourage a personal sense of identity for each person in a relationship and value authenticity. Catalysts have been known to get others into counseling and encourage them to transform their lives. Their feelings don't stop at sympathy; they seek the understanding that comes from empathy.

In college I was living at home and didn't like my parents always checking on me. I decided to move out and prove I

*am responsible. I wanted my own sense of identity. I achieved
well and am proud of my accomplishments. My parents
are, too, and our relationship has become better than ever.
It helped me grow and it helped my parents realize they
couldn't control me forever. Now we have a great relationship, and I know my moving out was the reason why.*

(INFJ)

*I have become very good friends with my coworker's two
daughters: April is five years old and Karen is seven. Almost
immediately, we became good friends. We all lived on site
and were neighbors. The girls loved to play over at our place
with my husband and me. They would rather have dinner at
our house and sleep at our house, and would go practically
anywhere with us. I could not figure out why until our relationship strengthened and then Karen confided in me. She
told me that her father always yelled at them and abused
their mother. This was so devastating to me that I immediately confronted their father. It was an extremely delicate
situation. First of all, I did not witness this myself, and second, it was not my business. But after Karen told me this, I
remembered seeing bruises on both of the girls also. I was
very traumatized by the thought of someone hurting these
precious little girls, but I did not know what I should do
next; I had never had to deal with a situation quite like
this before. I made several phone calls and talked to a lot
of different professionals to help assess the situation. The
entire family ended up in counseling, both individually and
together. They have been working through some very rough
times, but I can really see a difference in each and every
one of them. I am very thankful that Karen felt comfortable
enough to confide in me. My husband and I still maintain
the closeness of our relationship with April and Karen,
but do not really have any type of relationship with their
parents anymore.* (ENFP)

I made a decision to have the rights of my father's living will respected. I requested that my family and a panel of doctors discuss the case. My father was extremely ill and did not want to live on a ventilator. The doctors wanted to track him and send him to a rehab center on life support. I requested a CAT scan to see if he had suffered a stroke. He had, and it was his third. He was unable to eat, had no control over his bodily functions, and was septic and unconscious. I got my family to agree to remove him from life support. He died three hours later. My father and I had talked about his wishes on this matter years earlier. I knew it was what he would have wanted, but it was difficult to suggest to my seven brothers and sisters and my mother, who thought we should keep trying to save him.   (ENFJ)

Theme 10: Searching for the Meaning of Life

Catalysts tend to want to know, "What's it all about?" They may use frameworks and belief systems to gain insight about things or help other people understand. They often try to get their family and friends to see the big picture.

In the past, I have coached a junior high baseball team for my church. This involves teaching these boys not only the skills to become better players but important lessons that can be used throughout different aspects of their lives (for example, to teach them respect). At this age some of the kids did not always respect their parents and sometimes each other. One of the ways we enforced this was by addressing their behavior when we noticed it, and at times would have them do sprints if they acted disrespectfully. Toward the end of the season we did not have these types of problems anymore. We also helped them understand the importance of teamwork and would often split the kids up that were friends, when we needed different skills, to get them used to

*performing with different kids. One of the rules for the warm-
ups was that they had to pair up with someone different
each day until they were paired with every player on the
team. I believe I had a positive influence on this group of
kids because they are now seniors in high school and still
playing together and should be ranked as one of the best
teams in the state within their class of school.*   (ENFJ)

*I was transformed through some personal growth seminars
to "live life powerfully and live a life you love." I have since
raised money for my aunt to take the seminar because she
wanted to gain what she saw her niece achieve. So I helped
my aunt transform her life like I did for myself.*   (INFJ)

*Currently I am in the hardest "love" relationship of my life.
A good friend from work is going through a hard time also.
We provide each other support. We both have trouble understanding the male version of the situations we face. Through
the MBTI analysis I realized so much. These guys think different. I shared my MBTI materials and the framework with
my friend, and we used them to figure out our significant
others. I have an understanding now that we aren't wrong
and neither are they. Then we learned about the attitudes,
values, and behaviors typical of how they are and thought
about how we are, and can we live this way with such con-
tradictory preferences. As for my friend, she and her guy are
getting along better. As for me, I'm going through a world
of changes and hope that through thinking through things
that many think are natural, I'm learning that no matter
what you are learning and what you mean, just say what
you mean and mean what you say and always stand for
what you believe, because you'll lose touch with yourself
if you don't.*   (ENFJ)

COMPARING CATALYSTS (NFs) TO OTHER CORE PERSONALITY TYPES

Not only are Catalysts not all alike, they also share some similarities with other core personality types. Generally characterized as making a difference by rallying people for a cause for the long-term benefit of an organization or society, Catalysts (NFs) share a preference for Feeling with Harmonizers (SFs—described in chapter 5). While both Catalysts and Harmonizers are likely to pay attention to people, aesthetics, and values—and are likely to want to avoid conflict unless the situation violates their values—Catalysts are more likely to focus on the group of people that may be affected over the long term by a situation and address the situation in a creative and systematic manner, while Harmonizers are likely to do that in a more step-by-step manner that focuses on helping individuals right away.

Catalysts also share a preference for Intuition (N) with Visionaries (NTs—described in chapter 7). Thus both Catalysts and Visionaries will have a longer-term and bigger-picture perspective on a situation or relationship in which they are trying to make a difference. However, Catalysts are more likely to emphasize people and values, while Visionaries are more likely to emphasize the logical interconnections that produce an objective and logical system solution.

Catalysts generally have the least in common with Stabilizers (STs—described in chapter 4). Catalysts are likely to have a longer-term focus than Stabilizers and have a more people-oriented set of concerns in a given situation. They may also tend to emphasize helping a generalized group of people over an individual or specific situation.

EXERCISES FOR CATALYSTS

Before you move on to chapter 7, complete exercises 10 and 11 to help you determine how likely you are to use the themes described in this chapter to make a difference in your work and relationships.

EXERCISE 10

Using Catalyst (NF) Characteristics to Make a Difference at Work

Rate the extent to which you are likely to use the Catalyst themes described in this chapter to make a difference in a work situation, on the following scale:

0 = Almost never
1 = Seldom
2 = Occasionally
3 = Frequently
4 = Almost always

1. **Reaching dreams** (encourage growth; promote long-term development; instill a sense of being part of something bigger; spread idealism)   0 1 2 3 4

2. **Seeing good in everyone** (celebrate diversity; avoid gossip; seek win-win solutions; find good ideas in opposing views)   0 1 2 3 4

3. **Facilitating communication** (possess public relations, marketing, image-making skills; translate for others)   0 1 2 3 4

4. **Rescuing groups of people** (advocate for a cause; advocate for others)   0 1 2 3 4

5. **Developing people's potential** (value personal growth; develop potential; facilitate learning)   0 1 2 3 4

6. **Developing belief/value systems** (personalize the organization's mission; emphasize benefits to the people)   0 1 2 3 4

7. **Promoting change through relationships** (motivate others to change in service of the big picture; promote togetherness)   0 1 2 3 4

continues

Exercise 10 cont'd

8. Being creative (promote new ways to deal with issues and state messages; emphasize aesthetics of workplace)   0 1 2 3 4

9. Providing inspirational motivation (inspire with enthusiasm, fun, passion, charisma; get others to enjoy the journey)   0 1 2 3 4

10. Helping people understand (enhance the organization's and individuals' growth and development; answer all questions)   0 1 2 3 4

Be sure to save these ratings because you will be asked to use them in the planning exercises in chapter 8.

EXERCISE 11

Using Catalyst (NF) Characteristics to Make a Difference in Relationships

Rate the extent to which you are likely to use the Catalyst themes described in this chapter to make a difference in a *relationship* situation, on the following scale:

0 = Almost never
1 = Seldom
2 = Occasionally
3 = Frequently
4 = Almost always

1. Being deeply emotional (show emotions freely; bond with others; emphasize the importance of situations)   0 1 2 3 4

2. Advocating for causes (produce a better world; try to rescue the community)   0 1 2 3 4

3. Creating fun (make life fun for others; produce surprise, be spontaneous)   0 1 2 3 4

continues

Exercise 11 cont'd

4. Helping others with their relationships (facilitate groups, counsel others; take insights from relationships)

0 1 2 3 4

5. Encouraging others to take risks (promote risk taking; get others to follow their heart's desires; boost self-esteem and self-confidence)

0 1 2 3 4

6. Being inspirational (energize others; convert others' beliefs; demonstrate charisma)

0 1 2 3 4

7. Using communication skills (show creative use of language; get the word out; use analogies and metaphors)

0 1 2 3 4

8. Growing in relationships (influence friends and family; get others to explore long-term implications of relationships; assess worthiness of relationships)

0 1 2 3 4

9. Showing empathy, not just sympathy (honor will of others; encourage their sense of identity; value authenticity; seek true understanding)

0 1 2 3 4

10. Searching for the meaning of life (use a framework and/or belief system to understand; get friends to see the big picture)

0 1 2 3 4

Be sure to save these ratings because you will be asked to use them in the planning exercises in chapter 8.

How "Visionaries" (NTs) Can Make a Difference

People with preferences for Intuition (N) and Thinking (T) tend to be big-picture oriented and analyze interrelationships to help develop a blueprint for the future. We will refer to these NT types as "Visionaries." If you have determined by looking at the middle preferences of your four-letter MBTI type that you are a Visionary (that is, an NT), this chapter is especially for you. You may also want to read this chapter to learn more about others who have this core personality type.

We'll start with a "scouting report" on people with this core personality type and then move to a more detailed description of these and other tendencies reported in the research studies.

Scouting Report on Visionaries

Visionaries tend to . . .

- Search for interrelationships of possibilities through impersonal analysis
- Be calculative risk takers
- Constantly challenge themselves and others to reach higher levels of achievement

continues

Catalysts cont'd

- Come across as confident and blunt and as critical thinkers
- Want to be the architects of progress by being big-picture planners and problem solvers
- Prefer just enough structure in a situation to ensure productivity
- Be strategic, theoretical, and systematic
- Be goal and future oriented
- Be comfortable with and even prefer complexity
- Demand high standards of competence for themselves and others

Overall, Visionaries tend to make a difference . . .

- **At work** by emphasizing big-picture goals and offering their competencies to solve problems toward achieving goals
- **In relationships** by using logic and perspective to help people make plans and solve problems

A MORE DETAILED LOOK AT VISIONARIES

Once more, be sure to keep in mind that the descriptions of Visionaries that follow reflect general tendencies only. They are not true for all people with preferences for Intuition and Thinking. Furthermore, people with any of the other three core personality types could be found to exhibit the characteristics provided in the descriptions because situations—as well as personality preferences—drive behavior. Nevertheless, in general, these descriptions will help in your understanding of this core personality type.

Visionaries tend to prefer to focus their attention on possibilities and handle these with an objective, impersonal analysis of the options. At their best they tend to be logical and ingenious. They often figure things out quickly and understand how some things interrelate with other things. As a result, they may come across as theoretical, strategic, or even academic. Visionaries see abstract patterns more than singular details and immediately look for cause-and-effect relationships in those patterns. They are often more at home at work or in deep technical discussions. They may tend to focus on theoretical and technical issues first and human issues second. Research indicates that they are overrepresented among those having a "type A" personality.

Visionaries often prefer structured, quantifiable data. They may encourage the use of surveys to gather such data rather than merely identifying trends from anecdotal comments. Once they understand the ins and outs of their job, they may lose interest in following structured, step-by-step procedures and attempt to turn over administrative and implementation responsibilities to others. They are at their best at solving problems in their field of special interest.

Visionaries are likely to prefer to work in an organization that is goal-oriented and uses innovative, big-picture, future-oriented strategies. They tend to be calculative risk takers, seeking the challenge of greater achievement while understanding the odds underlying the options. Thus, they distinguish risk taking from gambling. As leaders, they are often plan formulators who want and need plan executors on their staff. They are often restless for change and want to move on to identify the next set of problems to conquer. They are more likely to think about what the organization could or should be than to feel satisfied with how it is now.

Visionaries like to analyze the organization they work for and are often interested in information about the organization's structure. They tend to prefer open organization environments rather than bureaucracies; but they want to see enough structure in the organization to encourage and ensure productivity, while allowing individuals the flexibility to be able to use their strengths. Thus, they may encourage a complex, contingency-based structure that is not all that clear to others. Likewise, they tend to set up procedures that are flexible in format but rational in content. They use procedures and their own intuition to gather information quickly and use it to gain a sense of progress. In a leadership position, Visionaries strongly emphasize progress and achievement. They will even work behind the scenes to move the organization in that direction. They often contribute to their organization by providing a research and theoretical foundation for the work being done.

Visionaries often come across as confident, revolutionary, blunt, and impersonal. They like to ask the question "Why?" a lot. At their best they want to be the architect of progress through the use of theories, research, models, and frameworks. They tend to have high expectations of themselves and of others, but they can work with almost anyone as long as they see that person as competent. They can become either very critical or very disappointed if they are asked to work with people less competent than themselves.

Their core values include achievement, change, innovation, and competency. While they may need to be praised for their competency, they may forget to do so for others. They can come across as quite competitive and critical. As leaders, Visionaries tend to escalate their standards across time. So when they ask for a subordinate to solve problem X and that person comes back with only a solution for problem X, they may actually appear disappointed. They really wanted the person to come back not only with that solution but also with exciting new ways the solution could provide intriguing possible solutions to problems Y, Z, and others. They also are impatient with repeated mistakes. They understand that anyone may make a mistake once but find it like "fingernails on the blackboard" if they encounter that person making the same mistake again.

Visionaries like to find ways to link systems, strategies, and models. They don't take things for granted, so they are likely to study solutions to complex problems. They tend to engage in debates, challenging the thinking of others with questions, critiques, and a request for evidence. They don't like to do other people's work and especially don't like to perform repetitive or administrative tasks.

Many of the tendencies described above also show up in Visionaries' personal relationships as well. Their penchant for problem solving may have them developing strategies rather than listening to others. Their expectations for challenge, competency, achievement, and growth will either be a blessing or a curse for their partners. They often make a difference in personal relationships in what others may view as impersonal ways.

HOW VISIONARIES (NTs) TEND TO DIFFER

Of course, not all Visionaries are alike. For example, the tendencies described above of NTs with a preference for Introversion (INTs) may be more difficult to see. They bring the world inside their own thought system. They may come across as impersonal because they want to think things through before responding. They may be the ones who are more likely to work independently behind the scenes. NTs with a preference for Extroversion (ENTs) tend to push overtly for change. It is clear what their thoughts and opinions are because they just tell you rather than waiting to be asked. They demand action and are likely to be juggling a lot of projects all at the same time.

NTs that have a preference for Judging (NTJs) are likely to be take-charge leaders with a focus on bottom-line achievement. They will likely be the field marshals moving organizations or relationships to the next level. NTs with a preference for Perceiving (NTPs) have a tendency to want to study issues from many different angles. They can see and produce many options and possibilities. They want to understand the organization or the relationship perhaps even more than they want to decide what to do about things. They can see both sides of an argument and may even feel comfortable debating from either side, as well.

VISIONARIES (NTs) MAKING
A DIFFERENCE AT WORK

Let's look at how Visionaries, when using the strengths of their natural preferences, can make a difference at work. Each of the following themes represents characteristics expressed by Visionary participants from the research studies. Each theme is illustrated by stories written by the participants, with the storyteller's four-letter type provided at the end of each story.

Theme 1: Utilizing Competencies

Visionaries typically value their competencies as well as the competencies of others. They can often make a difference at work by capitalizing on a particular competency—for example, by catching on quickly to how to do a job or what a project needs—and thus help the organization succeed in that area. Visionaries also tend to want to achieve. For Visionaries with a preference for Judging (NTJs) this may be manifested as a desire for closure on big projects, while for those with a preference for Perceiving (NTPs) it may be the development of big projects. Visionaries are also likely to use metrics to confirm accomplishments.

> As a manager, developing goals and plans are routine occurrences. Assisting and mentoring the teams to reach the goals is another challenge. We set lofty stretch goals each year. The team needs guidance to prioritize efforts, focus on the process, and let the overall accomplishments come to fruition. The team is pushed at times and rewarded/ recognized accordingly. As an example, we set a goal of cost reduction last year of $1.7 million over the previous year actual with relatively flat sales, no top-line growth. By March, the team had slipped by a couple hundred thousand. I rallied the team, set actionable targets, assisted the team in mind-set changes, focused efforts on cost impact and benefits, and we all put in some extra hours. By June, we were ahead of the projected savings curve. We celebrated with a small recognition meeting, where I handed out personal Palm Pilots to each of the engineers with heartfelt thanks. Since then I have worked hard to help our leadership team regain focus on driving the metrics of the com-

*pany and not the costs. The latter is a result of the former.
I have also challenged them to prevent mistakes before
they happen. We develop potential failure mode and effects
matrices to determine what could possibly go wrong and
take action to prevent the occurrence prior to its inception.
If a problem does occur, I insist we use a systematic
approach to problem solving (the 8 Ds). Typically, issues
are handled swiftly, with all parties either satisfied or at
least understanding.* (INTJ)

*I work as a sales assistant for the VP of a financial services
firm. When I started seventeen months ago, my main
responsibilities were to update records and handle mass
meetings. I found the job tedious and extremely dull. One
day I decided to restructure my responsibilities independently and work on marketing for the VP's clients. I put
together marketing letters and cold-called prospective
clients. I wanted to prove to my boss that I had the competencies to be an effective assistant and help grow the
business. I was skeptical whether he would allow me full
responsibility for his marketing, so I hid my work from him
at first. Within four months we had grown our business 40
percent. My VP was very optimistic about my efforts and
commended me on the results. For the first time in almost a
year on the job, I felt as though I was making a difference.
To date our business has grown over 70 percent since I took
over the marketing responsibilities. I want to continue much
of the system I started but want to revitalize our strategy
again this year.* (ENTJ)

*I am a career counselor with a master's degree in educa-
tional psychology. In the past fifteen years I have worked
directly with over ten thousand individuals, helping them
pass their GED tests and helping them prepare to get back
in the workforce. I am very good at what I do and have won*

many awards. The strategies I have developed have resulted in a very high rate of success. I am a multitasker and have thought through the whole system of how we deliver our services to our clientele.   **(ENTP)**

Theme 2: Challenging Self and Others

Visionaries tend to like challenges, which enable them to utilize their competencies. They may also come across as challenging, especially of authority and current practices and/or thoughts. They may rebel, debate, or even take actions to make up for an inadequate boss. Many Visionaries are seen as being nontraditional or nonconformist. They can make a difference by helping people at work think "outside the box."

I was working in Germany as an importer of construction materials. I was paired to work with a guy who had driven off more than his share of female associates. I stood up to him at work, and he developed grudging respect for me. I later found out he was also relatively nice to my replacement (another female), so maybe I changed his attitude in the long run.   **(INTP)**

I was transferred to a new branch with a new manager. I had met this manager a few times prior to working for him, and we had a pretty solid relationship. All of this would change from the day I started working for him. We both had a different way of doing the same thing. He was very set in his ways; all of his other employees were people who did whatever he said exactly how he said to do it. This manager did an OK job of running his branch. We all got paid on how much net profit the branch made. I had done some things that could make us even more money (all ethical and moral). He could not handle this. I finally had to sit him down and let him know why I was doing what I was doing.

*This manager finally saw what I was trying to do and he
eventually gave me a little more room to do my job.* (ENTJ)

*There was a difference of opinion between me and another
supervisor. The outcome of this decision would have a great
impact on how we deliver services to our clients seeking
employment and how employers might use our services. I
wrote a lengthy memo in support of my opinion to the director of these departments and to the associate director of
the agency. This put me in a very vulnerable position with
the other supervisors. However, I felt very strongly about the
decision, its outcome, and how we would serve the community. The memo caused the agency to conduct a survey
among all staff involved in this service, and the results
supported my opinion. It is nice to have support of your
opinion, and it increased my self-confidence in the way
I work.*   (ENTJ)

Theme 3: Being an Architect of the Future

Visionaries tend to be future oriented. They often develop and
design new systems, procedures, plans, or even goals for the business in a logical manner. Their plans will typically take into account
the interactivity of the elements of the systems they design.

*I came up with a strategy for selling credit cards in the
bank in China where I worked. I decided to call my VIP
customers and visited their offices and got them to apply
for a credit card. When they said it was a good product, I
went back and talked to their employees and friends and
signed them up too. My approach was listed as a model in
our training from that point on.*   (ENTJ)

*In the late seventies, I was hired by a national association
of faith groups to organize a coalition of organizations that*

provided food to poor people and churches that wanted to support them financially. I learned how to get a wide variety of types of people and organizations together for a common purpose. I also wanted the organization to deal much more with systemic causes of hunger and poverty than most of its founders. I got the organization started but did not continue my relationship with it. I left because the majority did not want what I wanted. The good news: The organization still survives as a coalition of food providers with ecumenical support and with substantial public dollars.

(INTJ)

I made a difference at work by changing the process by which we hang sale signs. Individuals used to hang the sign packet by themselves. This would include tearing the signs apart and then hanging them. This process took about six hours to do. I decided to make cashiers tear apart the signs during their free time (in-between customers). They tore the signs and organized them by aisle. I had the closing crew hang all sale signs on Saturday nights after the store was closed (as opposed to Sunday mornings during business hours). In all, the process now takes about two hours. This new process has also helped increase sales on Sunday mornings because customers are aware of sales without needing to consult the weekly ad.

(INTJ)

Theme 4: Taking Charge of Change Efforts

Many Visionaries report feeling compelled to lead—whether leading complex turnaround efforts by taking charge and making decisions (especially the ENTJs) or making concerted efforts to influence things by working behind the scenes (especially the INTs). In either case this compulsion is likely to be self-initiated rather than involve waiting for a boss to ask them to provide their knowledge and perspective.

I once had to help implement a major change effort at my previous job as general manager of a bakery/restaurant. We used to make the bakery items from scratch. This involved finding people willing to work the midnight shift, which is when the baking occurred. While the scratch baking was tasty, it involved lots of time, experienced bakers, and a lack of flexibility. The company moved to a totally different baking approach, which involved speed bake ovens. This also meant retraining the bakers on totally new ways of doing things. The bakers had to change their availability, and the new process involved more willingness to do a variety of jobs than the old process. I gave as much information as possible to the bakers to try to smooth the transition. But despite the preparations the process started on shaky ground, mainly because of our store layout. The process needed more time. I had to work with the bakers to develop adaptations to the process and then sell the changes to the corporate managers. The bakers were on the verge of quitting, but we worked through it. It went a lot smoother when everyone started listening to each other. **(INTP)**

In a work setting of 250 people at two facilities, I was hired as a new supervisor of a much-dismantled career development department of eight professional staff. I led in a way to turn this group into a team. I established weekly staff meetings to share the resources we were using with clients. We eventually developed a common approach with clients and a common resource directory, plus a specialized workbook to be used in individual or group settings. Since the workbook was to be produced by the clerical department, I initiated an effort to work with their supervisor so we would work better together. She was a real challenge. She wanted to make sure she was in charge of all work assignments. My getting her to buy in to working on our workbook was a real coup. Never before did the career development department

*have the support of their supervisor in becoming an entity
on its own.*   **(ENTJ)**

*I have changed my own role. I don't really like the adminis-
trative aspect of my job (which is difficult since my job title
is administrative assistant). So I started doing more research
and marketing functions. My supervisor recognized my
other skills and now offers me the chance to work on different projects.*   **(ENTP)**

*When our unit was in need of a union president, I volun-
teered to step in and complete the stalled negotiations.
Within three months we were able to hammer out a tentative agreement, which the membership ratified with a 100
percent vote to accept. This was a major accomplishment
given the differing factions within the union. I feel that my
listening and providing each group an opportunity to voice
their concerns and issues is what made the difference for
our group. I steered them to focus on issues instead of people, which they were not used to doing.*   **(ENTJ)**

Theme 5: Applying Knowledge

Visionaries typically not only value knowledge but also want to
deploy the theories and models they know are backed by suffi-
cient research data. They tend to want to see their perspectives
and education put to use. They may also be willing to do the
research required to produce the knowledge.

*I work as a custodian. I applied what I had learned in school
about "lean" production in order to improve things at work.
When another custodian is off, the custodians that are present have to cover that person's area. One day Nick was off
or called in, I have no idea, but he wasn't there. Nick had
problems in his area regarding his work. The clients com-*

plained when their areas weren't cleaned right, and Nick just didn't do a good job. Well, I was assigned to help cover—his closet was a mess. I had learned last semester that lean production all starts with cleaning up your work area. So I cleaned up his closet, restocked supplies, and not too soon after that Nick started doing better work in his area. **(ENTJ)**

I learned a technique called "planned spontaneous recognition" in one of my classes. I began to realize that I tend to take people's good work for granted. It made perfectly logical sense to me that reinforcing the behaviors that I want would result in more of these behaviors. I began practicing planned spontaneous recognition by bringing people together and praising the talent that I saw put to use. When I take the time to write an e-mail of appreciation, in depth, to the person helping me and to his or her manager, the results are 100 percent a blessing. That person always gives me better support in the future, and his or her manager has done the same. Everyone wins with planned spontaneous recognition. **(ENTJ)**

I was invited to join a team/committee that is considering ways to improve and develop economic growth in my city. This group didn't have a lot of structure. I suggested that we use the seven processes of great teams to improve our team. It was received with open arms. People were so pleased to know that we don't just have teams for social gatherings, but to really produce something. This group met in the past, where they shared dirty laundry, played the blame game, and had no real direction other than to dump on people. The point that I'm making is that I was an outsider and, frankly, knew that I would find it difficult to gain respect and to make a difference. I was bringing in a plan to get

*something done that this group had not considered, the
steps of making a great team.*

*This team is already starting to show results. It used the
first process to really establish a focus on what the team
wants to accomplish. Before, everyone always discussed
why things were broken, but without a clear direction, no
one focused on how to fix things. Next, the group began
to discuss who has the talent or contacts to make things
happen. Recruiting talented members was a natural pro-
gression after setting a clear direction! I then suggested
a brainstorming session on what talent is required to help
in defining what and who may be adding to the group.
Currently the group is actively searching for individuals
who can meet the team's talent needs. I plan to get the
group to then take a look at the rest of the seven steps
of what successful teams do.* (ENTJ)

Theme 6: Motivating Others by Setting High Standards

Visionaries tend to set high standards for themselves and others.
They may push colleagues and subordinates to settle for nothing
less than high achievement and believe this will motivate everyone to produce. Even when they have stated what they would like
to see others achieve, they often escalate those standards as the
project and the work get under way.

*Success comes from making a goal. Success comes from
being number one in the district. But the times when I feel
that I have really made the most difference come long after
these goals are reached. It comes from the praise from my
past managers years later when they tell me how much I
taught them. Recently one manager told me that I taught
him how to be professional and that he was able to have
his choice in jobs because I taught him key skills when he
worked for me. I also helped a manager by putting her on*

a career development plan because I saw her potential. She later was placed in a store where she greatly increased the sales volume and received further promotions. She thanked me for the difference I made in her life.   (ENTJ)

A couple of years ago I was working in a repair shop. I had been working there for about three years and knew everyone there pretty well. One day my supervisor told me in passing that everyone's evaluations were going to go down if we could not get motivated. I told him that I would organize a group discussion for the work center if he would let me run it, and that he wouldn't attend. Anyway, I got everyone together and told them the situation. Then I told them that each person was going to get a chance to answer why we were not motivated. I ran the meeting and asked every person the same questions, which they each answered in front of the group. By the end, everyone realized that as a group we had been slacking off, but that none of us really wanted to. There was a visible improvement in our group's motivation over the next few weeks, and the working environment was more enjoyable. This experience made me want to become an officer to lead people to make positive change.   (ENTJ)

I made a difference in a former coach and mentor's life. I played my entire junior year with a herniated disc. After the season he asked me why I kept playing (and leading the team in points scored and rebounds). I told him that I played because I could. Some people never get to play basketball or even walk. I love to compete. I am blessed enough to play and still have the will. In my mind, the only way I won't play is if I got shot. Later the coach told me that I changed the way he coached, and he mentions me in 98 percent of his speeches.   (ENTJ)

Theme 7: Solving Problems with Long-Term Fixes

Many Visionaries report engaging in analysis aimed at solving problems once and for all. They may make a difference at work by making sure their team doesn't settle for treating the symptoms of a problem and end up experiencing repeated mistakes. Visionaries typically are willing to conduct the needed research. NTs with a preference for Perceiving (NTPs) are likely to readily provide options, while those with a preference for Judging (NTJs) are likely to push for decisions.

> *I used my problem-solving skills on a problem that we were having at work. We were having too much inventory piling up in our back room. So I got us to sit down as a team and come up with a solution to the problem. Our solution consisted of putting our entire inventory into a back stock gun. So then when we went to order that specific item it told us that we had it in our back room. After ordering we could print out a pick list. An employee would then find that item in the back room and stock it on the shelf. I liked the solution we came up with because it not only solved the problem with one particular part missing but all of our parts.*
>
> (INTJ)

> *A situation that worked well for me was a time that I spent eight months at a customer location just running trials to identify the root cause of numerous problems. I felt that I had made a lot of good cases on all the issues to prove the root cause of the customer issues. Then we all sat down with management at both plants. No matter how much data I had, many of the key managers argued against my conclusions. I felt the wind was pushed from my sails. Just when I felt that all was lost, the customer engineer spoke up and supported my claims and the trustworthy nature of the trials and the results that I produced. With this one comment the tide changed, and I took away from this one situation*

that there is a balance of how you solve problems and who you have supporting your analysis that makes you effective.
(ENTJ)

A software project was failing because the procedures it required of the user were too complex. I found a clever solution that served the project. I've done this more than once.   (ENTJ)

It was this one particular time at work, when my coworker and I were working together. He blamed me for something that I didn't even have a clue about. The situation erupted over some defective parts that were produced on our side of the assembly line. The problems could only have came from our particular area, where both of us were working at the time. So it was either he or I who basically screwed up. The QC manager came along and inspected the parts and determined they were defective. He wanted to know what happened, and my coworker simply blamed it on me, which I found to be untrue. So I suggested an explanation of what happened. So from my coworker implicating me for creating a problem, I suggested something that managers could do to alleviate these problems in the workplace. Now it is stan-dard policy for employees to add input to processes to better accommodate the transformation process.   (INTJ)

Theme 8: Giving Expert Advice

Visionaries are often willing to give (or receive) advice as long as it is based on expertise. They can help make a difference in work settings by being willing to consult on projects, mentor high-potential new employees, and advocate for solutions by convincing others with their expertise.

My job as a parking valet requires decent people skills to make decent money. I find that I am always reminding my coworkers that the more they are nice and courteous toward people, the better tips they'll receive. Since many different types of people come to the hospital because it is ranked so high, I have to remember that not all people understand or accept United States values and practices. A lot of my coworkers get mad when some foreign people don't tip. When I hear these thought patterns occur, I remind them that these folks are new to the country, and they aren't totally familiar with the practices of this country. Then I ask my coworkers how well would they fare in another country. This question usually puts things back into perspective. **(ENTP)**

At my current job as a manager at a milling company, I do several things. One thing I always do is make sure everything is stocked. This is important because we as a staff do not want to have to stop in the middle of customer service or while we are doing other work to have to restock. With this job comes a lot of responsibility in the form of the knowledge I need to have. This is in regards to garden seeds, fertilizers, and all kinds of feeds. Many times I help customers in the spring and plan gardens, and decide what to use for fertilizer. This is something very personal to people, and I feel like it really affects their lives through the spring and summer every day. Specifically, earlier this year in the spring I was filling a seed order for a very loyal longtime customer. This fellow had always planted a green bean called Bush Blue Lake. He mentioned that it hadn't produced like he had hoped the year before. I recommended another variety called Derby. I told him how it's a similar-tasting bean and was good for canning or freezing and was also a white bean. I explained that the main advantage is that it pro- duces at least twice as much as the other. So he tried it and later in the summer he came back one day for the usual fall fertilizer and winter rye he buys. When I saw him, he told me how well the Derby beans did and he was really happy

about it. And that they tasted good, and were good for
canning, and his wife and family liked them as well. He
was really happy about it, and I was glad for him and I
felt good that I was able to help him.   (INTJ)

I provided a "Big 6" accounting firm with statistical evidence
to change their hiring practices and this led to more women
being considered for partner status with the firm.   (ENTP)

Theme 9: Looking at the Big Picture

Visionaries at their best tend to see quickly how things connect.
They may expand the scope of projects and look for implications
beyond their own department and/or organization. Visionaries are
often interested in planting seeds for change but already envision
what the final product should turn out to look like.

I make travel arrangements for the VP of development.
He was used to receiving his flight itinerary along with his
ticket. I began to provide travel and meeting agendas, as
well as an executive summary of the company he is meeting
with. I assembled the information in a clear and logical for-
mat and put the packet in a clear plastic folder. This holistic
package was a lot easier to take on flights and provided
reading materials for travel times. Also, the VP is more
educated when walking into the meeting.   (ENTP)

I was assigned to a project in a law firm. The two colleagues
I had to work with were real detail oriented. I was able to
help them create a structured framework that helped them
sort out the priorities and accomplish their tasks on time.
This project required long hours and brought into the open
a lot of conflict. I maintain my cool under pressure and
handle stress and lack of sleep exceptionally well. This also
helped me keep the clients focused and still keep things in
perspective.   (ENTP)

*The other day at work I and another sales associate had
a meeting with management about what we as associates
were doing wrong when it comes to customer service. Instead,
I gave my manager analysis of what the store was doing
wrong and how that affected customer service more than
individual associates. My friend and I joke about that being
our first consulting job.* **(ENTP)**

*We have an ongoing project to enhance our procedures and
analyze how we affect each other's departments. The team
consists of a key member from seven different departments.
We then meet once a week to find out how well we have
accomplished our to-do list; then we discuss how each
department needs to use the data and what we will do or
find out the next week. I have found this group to be very
effective because we have decided to do nothing until
everyone agrees.* **(ENTP)**

Theme 10: Mediating Disputes

Visionaries are typically comfortable with conflict as long as the
conflict is ultimately dealt with on logical, not emotional, grounds.
They often make a difference at work by staying calm during disputes and serving as a mediator or go-between with parties who
are at odds with each other.

*I've made a large difference at work by being the middle-
man between the boss and employees. My boss is a longtime
friend. She doesn't always connect with the employees, and
vice versa. I am able to communicate effectively between
them because I understand what they both are feeling and
thinking.* **(ENTP)**

*On numerous occasions I've acted as an intermediary
between my coworkers and my restaurant owner. People
at my job look to me to ask questions and convey concerns*

to our boss. Many of my coworkers are afraid of my boss,
whereas I am not. For example, when one of my coworkers
had a major blowout with my boss, I acted as a buffer. I've
also acted as the main person to deal with for customer
relations. Everybody at my job usually will come to me
if they have a problem arise with customers (for example,
if food is sent back or a customer has complained about
service).   (INTJ)

I do a lot in joint union–management settings. I try to make
it clear that they will never agree on everything. They need
to look at which issues are of mutual interest. Then they
need to stay away from the blame game and figure out
what to do rather than spend all that time trying to figure
out who is at fault. Eventually they realize that they waste
a lot of time finding fault and are both better off when they
look at it as problem solving.   (INTP)

VISIONARIES (NTs) MAKING A DIFFERENCE IN RELATIONSHIPS

Now let's look at how Visionaries, when using the strengths of their natural preferences, can make a difference in their personal relationships.

Theme 1: Making a Personal Difference Impersonally

Visionaries might describe relationships as a task they really care about, and to which they proudly bring their competencies to bear in an effort to make a difference. Their natural tendency toward logic, achievement, and a focus on the future may lead them to address relationship issues in a blunt and forthright manner. They have seen their strengths work elsewhere. Why not employ those strengths with the people they care about for the sake of the relationship?

I established trust in a relationship with a significant other by using my systematic planning skills. I thought about what a girl might want on an ideal date. I then planned where to take her to dinner, bought her flowers, took her out to the movies, and served her breakfast in bed. **(INTJ)**

After my father passed away, I took on a more important role in my mother's life. I became the consultant for decisions. She asked me to help repair things or coordinate repairs as needed. Through this our relationship has become stronger and it has drawn us closer together. I hope my mother feels valued by my actions and concern for her well-being. **(INTJ)**

I help my family and friends by helping them to see how what they are doing fits into the broader context of their lives. This often involves articulating their thoughts, fears, and ideas more clearly than they are able to do on their own. The point of these efforts is to help them achieve their fullest potential. That is what drives my own actions regarding my own future. Making a difference in a relationship is really all about perspective and potential. **(ENTP)**

Theme 2: Problem Solving and Planning

Visionaries can make a difference in relationships by helping to figure things out. Others can often personally benefit from their natural abilities in problem solving and planning. NTs with a preference for Perceiving (NTPs) may be likely to provide analysis and options, whereas those with a preference for Judging (NTJs) may push for decision making and closure.

My extended family is spread out all over southeastern Michigan. There are fourteen grandchildren that never got to visit our grandparents. For their fiftieth wedding anniversary, I arranged for a "grand-kid" photo. It was next to

*impossible for all of us to get together, but I was able to
coordinate schedules and find a studio large enough to
accommodate us. The picture turned out great, and my
grandparents were so happy to see that we had all come
together for them.*   (ENTP)

*One story that comes to mind is something that has hap-
pened two or three times. My neighbor two doors down is
about eighty years old. She keeps in contact with certain
relatives mostly through instant messaging and e-mail.
When she first got on the Internet she had a problem
installing the program, and her computer was acting up,
too. She called my house and asked if I could help. I went
over and solved the problems without too much difficulty.
She offered to pay me, but I turned it down. I told her that
my family knew her for a long time and she had done us
favors in the past, such as taking care of our dog when we
were away. More recently she had a problem again with her
Internet service provider and called me, and I helped her fix
it again. She's a nice old lady, and I realize I probably saved
her a lot of frustration and stress. The fact is, most people
her age would never even use the Internet and a computer,
so she is doing all right.*   (INTJ)

*During high school I had a group of friends who were very
close for many years. When high school ended, we all got
somewhat separated and busy. So I started a softball team
for all of us to play on. Through this we all got a chance to
get together twice a week as a team. I think this helped us
all stay close over the years.*   (INTP)

Theme 3: Encouraging Independence and Self-Reliance

Visionaries tend to be self-reliant. People in a relationship with an
NT may be able to count on that person to do what is needed and

to do it on their own. Visionaries may be able to envision what their partner wants and tend to embody the concept that "it is better to give than to receive." Thus, they often contribute to a relationship by being "low maintenance."

> *I am the fourth of ten children. At age ten I was placed into foster care due to child neglect. I grew up and made a way for myself financially and then gained guardianship of my four youngest siblings. I raised them myself so they could be with the rest of their brothers and sisters out of foster care.*
> **(INTP)**

> *In relationships, I have been the "dumper" instead of the "dumpee," but for some reason my ex-boyfriends will contact me the day that my successive relationships end to try to renew the relationship I had with them. I don't know why. When I got married, I received several cards with "Congratulations, if it doesn't work out, I can be reached at. . . ." I am convinced this has nothing to do with my looks. I have come to the conclusion that my tendency to laugh at the stupid things men do rather than get emotional, snappish, or silent is what makes them comfortable with me. I am also blunt and don't play games. Maybe that's it.* **(INTP)**

> *I supported my wife to start and build a successful training business both by providing encouragement and giving her space to go beyond my wants and needs.* **(ENTP)**

> *I recently ended my relationship with my "army guy." He is going back to Iraq for the third time and told me that he has a girlfriend near his base there. Although this hurts, I listen to all his feelings that he can't sort out, even though he does not reciprocate when I talk about my mixed feelings about my new "manfriend." I know he can't give as much as he takes now, but in the past he gave more than he took. So*

now I do my best to duplicate that for him in his time of
need. (ENTJ)

Theme 4: Helping Others Increase Their Competence

Visionaries typically value competence, their own as well as that
of others, and often encourage others to continue to develop their
knowledge base and skills. Instead of simply stating, "I feel you
could develop," they may provide logical plans for developing competencies and resources, such as financial support.

> *I was working on a group project with two other students*
> *about a year ago. We had to do about a twenty-minute pre-*
> *sentation with visual aids. I am very comfortable in public*
> *speaking situations but also understand that many people*
> *are not. I encouraged the other two members of my group to*
> *step up, speak out, and really take charge during the presen-*
> *tation. I was supportive, suggesting ideas and then letting*
> *them run with those ideas. Our presentation was well put*
> *together and rehearsed (just enough so we weren't too stiff!).*
> *On the day we presented I was so proud of my two other*
> *group members. Sure, they seemed a little nervous at first,*
> *but once they got going they seemed poised. After the pre-*
> *sentation was over, they both commented that they felt more*
> *confident speaking in front of a group of people.* (INTJ)

> *I have made a big impact with my current girlfriend. Her*
> *freshman year of college she skipped class and did really*
> *bad in school. When we first started dating I encouraged*
> *her to do well in school and impressed on her that it is very*
> *important to get an education. I basically told her in this*
> *time and age you need a good education to have a good-*
> *paying job and a happy life. I still give her tons of encour-*
> *agement and motivate her as much as possible, and now*
> *she is doing better than I am in school. She is pulling a 4.0,*
> *while I get 3.0s.* (INTJ)

I am the "voice of reason" in most of my relationships. I have become quite the "life coach." For example, my husband and I recently visited an attorney to update our wills. The female lawyer was nice, competent, and businesslike. A week later I returned alone to review the documents with her, and we finished business very fast but then spent the next two and a half hours just talking. She is now determined to obtain a PhD in geriatric counseling based on the reflective listening I provided her. (INTP)

Theme 5: Using Relationship Skills Learned Formally

Visionaries often like to figure things out. Thus, they may logically try to determine the interpersonal skills required to enhance the relationships they desire. They tend to like to learn. Learning to listen, learning to pick their battles and not debate everything, and learning other relationship skills from outside sources such as books may be a pathway for them to grow and develop themselves and their relationships.

In a relationship I have made a difference by learning how to be a good listener and negotiator. Time after time I used to find myself not listening and somewhat ignoring the feelings expressed by my girlfriend. She always said I didn't listen and that I ignored her. I saw this as a personal competency problem more than a relationship problem, so I started to repeat things she would say and feelings she expressed, and I would repeat them back to her. This resulted in she and I understanding what was being communicated, so no one would jump to conclusions and lash out simply because of a miscommunication. Also, I learned how to express feelings in a different manner. I found that some people are very sensitive to the way some words are used to communicate, and you have to watch it. I tended to communicate the way I felt in an openly blunt manner.

*This produced some truthful communications to some
extent, but the phrases I used also created problems. I
find myself addressing problems differently because of
this. Usually now I say "I felt like this because. . . ." This
helps the other party understand where I am coming from.*
(INTJ)

*I had a relationship with a girl for four years that had a lot
of conflict. She was not very confident and felt threatened
when I talked to other females. I tried to make adjustments
to avoid fights. I finally decided I needed to stand up for
myself. I needed to learn how to confront issues and not just
tiptoe around them. This resulted in the end of the relationship but helped me grow up personally. Sometimes in life
you have to put your needs ahead of what your heart tells
you to do to save a relationship. I am now a better student,
a better manager, and a better leader. I have found a new
girlfriend that I would never have met if I had stayed with
my regular patterns.*
(ENTP)

*When faced with conflicts with my girlfriend I am trying to
use what I learned in school about the styles of conflict
resolution. I will first try to compromise in hopes of us both
feeling satisfied. I have also learned to be very selective in
the battles I pick. I have found this strategy to be helpful in
work-related conflicts as well.*
(ENTJ)

Theme 6: Using High Standards to Motivate Others

Visionaries tend to set high standards for themselves. Just as they
often experience success using this strategy at work, they may
also set high standards in relationships and believe this will be a
motivating force. They may model self-reliance and thus encourage their partners to see that they can do many things on their
own.

Over the past three years, I have seen my husband earn three successful promotions. He has told me that my influence has directly contributed to his recent success. I try to be very supportive by asking questions about what he does (because I am truly interested) and by quizzing him about different paths his career may take. I also try to give him enough space to grow and thrive as an individual, not as an adjunct to me. I try to help him by example, too. I am naturally very bright, but I also work very hard and try not to "coast" on my natural abilities. My husband has said this quality of mine inspires him to do better as well. Even though we are at different stages in our professional lives—he having an established career and I still being a student— my actions and attitude level the playing field in our relationship.   **(INTJ)**

A few years ago, we were planning to join in on an extended family trip. We invited our niece and nephew to join us. Other family members took exception, wanting to keep our children's time devoted to playing with their children. As we saw it, there was plenty of time and people to entertain each other. There was no need for conflict. Rather than uninvite the children as demanded, we stood by our conviction that the vacation was just a tool to attain the family time we sought. We ended up vacationing separately that year with our guests, hopefully setting the role model position that you don't turn your back on family for an easy way out of avoiding conflict. We have had great relations with these children, partly I believe because the trust and respect was not broken during this event. When it comes to providing an ethical standard at work or at home, I somehow have come to be known affectionately as "Dudley Do-Right." Ethics are important, and looking out for the well-being of others is not just proper, it's the right thing to do. For instance, when receiv-

*ing change from a store, I always point out when they over-
pay me or underpay me. I believe in dealing in good faith.*

(INTJ)

*When I decided to enroll back in college, I set out to get all
As. I wanted to show my children that you can still get good
grades even when you have a lot going on in your life. Since
entering in 2004, I have completed forty-eight credit hours
with fifteen As and three A-minuses. This semester's twelve
credit hours are up in the air right now; however, I'm proud
to tell my children that right now my GPA sits at 3.54, and
I attended the honors banquet with my two daughters. The
other activities I engage in are working a full-time as well
as a part-time job, raising our four kids, my husband, the
housework, being a three-quarters to full-time student, and
acting as a liaison to our union and participating on the
negotiation team. Since I enrolled in college, all of my
children have made the honor roll!* (ENTJ)

*Many of my friends are caught up in the "street life." I try
to spark conversations with them about real issues (for
example, world news, business opportunities, societal values,
and so on). I try to spark their mind and give them confidence
in their thinking. I want them to understand that you don't
have to be in college to be intelligent or knowledgeable.*

(INTP)

*With people or in relationships outside of work I make a
difference by motivating others. First, I motivate younger
relatives by setting a standard high with my own results
(grades, staying employed, being responsible). I tell them
when they are doing good and let them know how proud
the family is of them. I promise and deliver money for fun
outings for good accomplishments. Second, I motivate*

boyfriends by boosting their ego, giving them lots of compliments and verbal and nonverbal rewards (for example, by buying something that's their favorite or letting them choose to do something they like). I praise them or speak about them doing great things or things I like, and in the end they usually conform to things that I have praised them for—they become those things. And I motivate peers by reminding them of their past achievements or of any benefits or rewards they might receive for their efforts. I will also try to help them or do it with them, and that way they don't feel alone and they can see and feel like they have support.

(ENTP)

Theme 7: Negotiating Conflicts

Visionaries tend to view interpersonal conflicts as just another problem to solve. They can contribute to relationships by staying calm when confronting the person about, and discussing, an issue. They may also help mediate disputes for friends and family members they care about.

When I left for college my parents were going through a very hard time in their relationship. By the end of my first year at school my stepmom had left home and moved into an apartment. When I found out, I came home and spoke with each one of them and found out that neither wanted to leave the relationship. I then decided that they should go out on a date with no pressures and just enjoy one another. They were having issues because they were trying to blend two families, but the two families had already grown but not together. They ended up getting back together after a few months of going out, just the two of them, and discussing with each other how to move forward.

(ENTP)

I stepped in as a liaison between my mother and brother as they got into arguments. I convinced my mother that her brother was strong enough not to be swayed by friends of questionable character. I convinced her that my brother is more likely to influence others than be influenced by them. I also told my brother, "This is your mother. She gave birth to you and cares about your well-being. She is only looking out for your best interests. You have to understand how your actions could upset her if you were in her shoes." I was able to show them the view that neither of them could see alone. The relationship is still rocky, but it has improved.   **(ENTP)**

When I first got married, there seemed to be a lot of quarrels between my husband and me. We even quarreled about the foods that I needed to prepare for the dinner. I was the person that liked to get the results from these quarrels— I had to know who was right and who was wrong. In my mind, the quarrel became a question about love. Then, we began to realize that we could not have these kinds of quarrels any longer. They were really unnecessary and they hurt our feelings. So we tried to avoid the conflicts about trivial things. Before, when I felt uncomfortable, I would speak out. But later, I just let myself calm down and wait at least two to three hours to think about it. After that, I didn't feel so bad. It was a good way to avoid trivial conflicts with someone important to you.   **(ENTJ)**

Theme 8: Using Logic in Clever Ways

Visionaries tend to have a creative side to their personality. However, the creativity may be more a cognitive function than an aesthetic one. They may help relationships by planning creative encounters or seeking smart ways to please others. Their use of puns and metaphors may bring a smile (or a groan) and stimulate conversations.

My best friend, Amy, was having trouble with her marriage. She and her husband, David, were threatening divorce every other day. They are a dramatic couple, but this was worse than usual. I asked Amy why she was getting so impatient with David, and she couldn't explain it. I told her how I felt when I got out of the navy. You feel like you have to decide your whole life by the day you get out, because if you don't have a plan, you'll definitely end up back in the military. It happens all the time. In some ways it's easier to sign your life away to Uncle Sam than to try to make it as a civilian. Especially after you've already been there and you know you can do it. A couple of days later she called me and told me that she and David were doing great after our talk. He had just gotten out of the navy last year and he understood my analogy totally. She said now when she feels like that they can talk about it, and he can calm her down before she makes an explosive decision.   **(INTJ)**

In relationships I find myself going out of my way to improve them. My girlfriend lives about two hours away, but I drive every weekend just to see her. One time I surprised my girlfriend and put her on a scavenger hunt by leaving a flower at various locations, each left with a note leading to the next location. I enjoyed figuring out the whole thing. I do little things like that to surprise my girlfriend.   **(ENTP)**

A couple of years ago I gave my wife an extra-special birthday gift. I am in the military, and we have to move around a lot. So, I arranged for my wife's mother to meet my wife at a spa. Her mother had never been and had always wanted to go, and my wife really enjoyed spending a day getting pampered and spending the whole time with her mother.

*They both really enjoyed the experience, and it made me
feel really good to have been a part of it.*   (ENTJ)

*In my freshman year I met my current boyfriend, Mike, but
at this time he was only a friend. It was late September and
it was his birthday, and he was going to spend it alone. A
friend and myself arranged for a group of friends to meet us
and then kidnapped Mike, blindfolded him, and drove him
downtown and surprised him for his birthday dinner. Next
we blindfolded him back up and surprised him with a trip
to the Tigers baseball game (his favorite sport). It was a
birthday he will never forget, even though at that point we
knew each other only a few weeks.*   (ENTJ)

Theme 9: Giving and Using Expertise

Visionaries tend to value expertise and achievement. Visionaries
with a preference for Judging (NTJs) especially may make a difference in relationships by giving sound advice or just getting things
done by themselves.

*I am the most educated in my family, so I help my parents
and brothers with a lot in life in general. I am the oldest
brother, so I tell my younger brothers to use me as a source
all through life, about girls, and so on. I help my parents
with finances, more specifically how to spend money wisely—
like buying a six-month-old car with extended warranties
and saving thousands of dollars they would waste on a
new car.*   (INTP)

*I make a difference in relationships when people ask me
for my advice. They don't have to take my advice. It is just
enough to know that they think I am important enough to
them to ask me for it.*   (ENTJ)

*My second wife and I negotiated our roles in the relation-
ship before we wed. We use our own experience as a model
for other couples planning to wed.*   (ENTP)

Theme 10: Taking a Big-Picture View

Visionaries naturally tend to look at the big picture. They help
friends and family gain a perspective. When it comes to relationships then, they may see themselves as part of a team dealing with
the demands of life. They can make a difference by increasing the
opportunities for growth, so they and their partner can create a
better life.

*My friend was about to make an unethical decision. She
wanted to put sugar in her ex-boyfriend's gas tank and
destroy his car. I reminded her of the fact that it could be
traced back to her and she could get in trouble, and then
how happy would he be to see her suffering over him and
then be punished for it? How humiliating would that be?*
                                                    (ENTP)

*Friends will comment that I seem to be in relationships
with people so different from me. I just would rather be with
people who can do things well that I could probably do but
not easily and not as well. For example, I can help my marriage by figuring out our finances, planning long-term stuff,
and being a caring voice of reason. My wonderful wife
enhances our lives by giving us a social life, wonderful food,
relaxing times, and getting me to just let go of work and
tasks and enjoy our love. We both add more than this to our
relationship, but these things sure make a difference.* (INTP)

*I always remind my friends of the two things I strive to
achieve every day. I tell them how much better I feel when
I am not worrying about things that I can't change. I always*

*tell them to smile, because it good for you because your
brain releases endorphins. I also remember once when my
sister was all worried over a test she was going to have to
take at the end of the semester. Here she was worrying and
it was the beginning of the semester. I reminded her that
she really was not gaining anything from all this worrying.
I reminded her that all she could do was to prepare herself
on a regular basis. She never had a problem with reminding
herself how well she has done on things. So at the end of the
semester she ended up getting an A in the class, and I felt
good about being a big brother. I felt proud that I was able
to listen to her and give her decent advice.*   **(ENTP)**

*I have a brother named Scott. He works hard driving a truck
over the road. He earns good money and owns many toys:
three cars, a snowmobile, a pickup truck, and a boat. He will
turn thirty this year and has not started to invest for his
retirement. I am thirty-two and have nearly $200,000
invested in various accounts. I have talked with Scott about
the importance of putting money away now. This last summer all the siblings sat down with our mother to go over her
estate so we would know what her wishes are and how she
would like things handled. During these sessions the others
realized that I owned a larger estate than my mother did
because she had not invested money in a long-term account.
Since then Scott has sold some of his assets to invest in
mutual funds . . . better late than never.*   **(ENTJ)**

COMPARING VISIONARIES (NTs) TO OTHER CORE PERSONALITY TYPES

Not only are Visionaries not all alike, they also share some similarities with other core personality types. Generally characterized as
doing even personal things in an impersonal manner and trying to set up systems for long-term solutions, Visionaries share a

preference for Thinking with Stabilizers (STs—described in chapter 4). Thus both Visionaries and Stabilizers may come across as somewhat impersonal when trying to make a difference because they both want to analyze, critique, and logically address the situation. Visionaries are likely to look for patterns and interconnections among the details and seek a system that addresses the long-term issues associated with the situation or relationship, while Stabilizers are more likely to focus on the specific details of the immediate situation one step at a time.

Visionaries share a preference for Intuition with Catalysts (NFs—described in chapter 6). Thus both types tend to bring a longer-term and bigger-picture perspective to the situation or relationship in which they are trying to make a difference. Visionaries will likely emphasize the logical interconnections that produce an objective and logical system solution, while Catalysts are more likely to emphasize people and values of the cause.

Visionaries generally have the least in common with Harmonizers (SFs—described in chapter 5). They tend to be some of the most self-reliant types and are likely to take an independent and impersonal—that is, logical—approach to solving the long-term problems associated with the work or relationship situation. Harmonizers are likely to value a relationship even more than an optimal solution to a given problem.

EXERCISES FOR VISIONARIES

Before you move on to chapter 8, complete exercises 12 and 13 to help you determine how likely you are to use the themes described in this chapter to make a difference at work and in your relationships.

EXERCISE 12

Using Visionary (NT) Characteristics to Make a Difference at Work

Rate the extent to which you are likely to use the Visionary themes described in this chapter to make a difference in a work situation, on the following scale:

0 = Almost never
1 = Seldom
2 = Occasionally
3 = Frequently
4 = Almost always

1. **Utilizing competencies** (focus on achievement; push for development; use knowledge and skills to get things done; use metrics to confirm accomplishments)   0 1 2 3 4

2. **Challenging self and others** (challenge authority; rebel, debate; be nontraditional, nonconformist; push for change)   0 1 2 3 4

3. **Being an architect of the future** (develop/design new systems, procedures, plans, goals)   0 1 2 3 4

4. **Taking charge of change efforts** (feel compelled to lead; make decisions; self-initiate; lead turnaround efforts)   0 1 2 3 4

5. **Applying knowledge** (put theories and models into practice; be willing to do research to produce knowledge)   0 1 2 3 4

6. **Motivating others by setting high standards** (push others to high achievement; escalate standards)   0 1 2 3 4

7. **Solving problems with long-term fixes** (use analysis to solve problems; conduct research; provide options; push for decisions)   0 1 2 3 4

continues

Exercise 12 cont'd

8. Giving expert advice (give advice; consult on   0 1 2 3 4
projects; mentor high-potential new employees;
advocate positions based on expertise)

9. Looking at the big picture (see how things   0 1 2 3 4
connect; look for external implications; envision
the whole package)

10. Mediating disputes (be comfortable with   0 1 2 3 4
conflict; act as go-between; stay calm during
disputes to negotiate a solution)

Be sure to save these ratings because you will be asked to use them in
the planning exercises in chapter 8.

EXERCISE 13

Using Visionary (NT) Characteristics to Make a Difference in Relationships

Rate the extent to which you are likely to use the Visionary themes
described in this chapter to make a difference in a *relationship*
situation, on the following scale:

0 = Almost never
1 = Seldom
2 = Occasionally
3 = Frequently
4 = Almost always

1. Making a personal difference impersonally   0 1 2 3 4
(be logic, achievement, and future oriented;
address issues forthrightly)

2. Problem solving and planning (analyze and   0 1 2 3 4
provide options; push for decisions and solutions)

continues

Exercise 13 cont'd

3. Encouraging independence and self-reliance   0 1 2 3 4
(be trustworthy; envision what partner wants; be
"low maintenance"; model independence)

4. Helping others increase their competence   0 1 2 3 4
(value competence; encourage others' development; provide logical plans)

5. Using relationship skills learned formally   0 1 2 3 4
(logically determine interpersonal skills required;
listen; pick battles; learn from outside sources)

6. Using high standards to motivate others   0 1 2 3 4
(uphold high standards; push others to achieve;
model self-reliance)

7. Negotiating conflicts (confront people and   0 1 2 3 4
issues; mediate disputes; stay calm)

8. Using logic in clever ways (plan creative   0 1 2 3 4
encounters; seek smart ways to please others;
use puns and metaphors)

9. Giving and using expertise (value compe-   0 1 2 3 4
tency and achievement; give sound advice;
get things done)

10. Taking a big-picture view (provide perspec-   0 1 2 3 4
tive; see relationship as a partnership)

Be sure to save these ratings because you will be asked to use them in
the planning exercises in chapter 8.

Planning to Make a Difference

We are what we repeatedly do. Excellence, then,
is not an act but a habit.
—ARISTOTLE

If you have not done so already, it is time for you to make use of
what you have learned from this book. Perhaps you have enjoyed
reading the stories, learning about your personality type, or thinking about ways you have made a difference at work or in relationships. This chapter provides a systematic process to help you make
use of your personality to increase the frequency with which you
make a difference. The process includes exercises for determining
your capability for making a difference, learning from your previous efforts, and planning next steps, both short-term and long-
term.

DETERMINING YOUR CAPABILITY FOR MAKING A DIFFERENCE

Just wanting to make a difference won't make it happen. As
described earlier, making a difference is a function of three elements: your abilities, your motivation, and your opportunities. You
can examine these three elements in any order, but you must put

them all together to create a plan for capitalizing on the strengths of your natural preferences and form the habits of making a difference at work and in relationships.

Your Abilities

Your personality preferences indicate something about your style. They don't necessarily describe what you are good at doing, just what may come more naturally to you. Let's focus first on your core personality type—that is, whether you have a preference for Sensing or Intuition, Thinking or Feeling. Are you a Stabilizer (ST), a Harmonizer (SF), a Catalyst (NF), or a Visionary (NT)? Review the exercises you completed in the specific chapter on your core personality type: Stabilizers, chapter 4, exercises 6 and 7; Harmonizers, chapter 5, exercises 8 and 9; Catalysts, chapter 6, exercises 10 and 11; and Visionaries, chapter 7, exercises 12 and 13. If you also completed exercises for core types other than your own, review those results as well. Use these results to complete exercise 14.

EXERCISE 14

Using Your Natural Abilities to Make a Difference

1. Work themes. From the ten "at work" themes described in the chapter on your core personality type, choose the three themes you feel you can use most naturally in your efforts to make a difference at work. The ratings you assigned the themes in the "at work" exercise in that chapter should help you decide, but feel free to use logic or your feelings to help you choose, both for your current work situation and for those situations you anticipate in the future. You are probably capable of using more than three of these themes, but it is important that you stayed focused on those.

a. _____

b. _____

c. _____

continues

Exercise 14 cont'd

2. Relationship themes. From the ten "in relationships" themes described in the chapter on your core personality type, choose the three themes you feel you can use most naturally in your efforts to make a difference in relationships. The ratings you assigned the themes in the "in relationships" exercise in that chapter should help you decide, but feel free to use logic or your feelings to help you choose, both for your current relationships and for those you anticipate in the future. You are probably capable of using more than three of these themes, but it is important that you stay focused on those.

a. _____

b. _____

c. _____

3. Past themes. Past behaviors are often good predictors of future behaviors. Review your responses in exercises 1 and 2, in chapter 2. Did you use any abilities to make a difference at work or in relationships in those events that you did not list in steps 1 or 2 above? If so, list those abilities below:

a. _____

b. _____

c. _____

4. Other themes. Review any ratings you assigned to the themes in the exercises in the chapters about core personality types other than your own. If you did not complete those exercises, review appendix C, which includes a full list of themes indicated for all four core personality types at work and in relationships. If one of these other approaches indicates abilities you would like to add to your "short list" to put to use in the near future, list each ability below.

a. _____

b. _____

c. _____

Your Motivation

Just because you are capable of making a difference doesn't mean you will take the initiative to do so. You also need to be motivated to use the natural abilities associated with your core personality type. Motivation is primarily a function of two things: expectations and rewards. Exercise 15 will help you think through what may motivate you to activate your abilities to make a difference.

EXERCISE 15

Your Motivation to Make a Difference

1. Past motivations. First, review your responses in exercises 1–3, in chapter 2. Identify below some of the things that motivated you on those occasions to make a difference at work or in relationships.

a. _____

b. _____

c. _____

d. _____

e. _____

2. Expectations at work. Expectations at work, either imposed on you by others or by yourself, might motivate you to make a difference. For example, managers are typically expected to clarify what work needs to get done and do so in a considerate manner. List below some of the things expected of you at work. Fulfilling which of those expectations might be an opportunity for you use your natural abilities to make a difference?

a. _____

b. _____

continues

Exercise 15 cont'd

c. _____

d. _____

e. _____

3. Rewards at work. Rewards at work can be external, such as gaining a promotion, a better workspace, or an increase in pay; or internal, such as getting recognition or enjoying a sense of accomplishment, efficacy, or power. Which rewards would make fulfilling the expectations you listed in step 2 worthwhile and motivate you to make a difference at work?

a. _____

b. _____

c. _____

d. _____

e. _____

4. Expectations in relationships. Expectations in your current relationships, either imposed on you by the other person or by yourself, might motivate you to make a difference. For example, some people expect their partners to check in regularly and let them know where they are going and when will they be coming home. List below some of the things expected of you in your relationships. Fulfilling which of those expectations might be an opportunity for you to use your natural abilities to make a difference?

a. _____

b. _____

c. _____

d. _____

e. _____

continues

Exercise 15 cont'd

5. Rewards in relationships. Rewards in relationships can be external, such as being able to spend more time with the other person or gaining a commitment of an exclusive relationship; or internal, such as knowing you are being the kind of partner you want to be or feeling you are being a good person. Which rewards would make fulfilling the expectations you listed in step 4 worthwhile and motivate you to use your abilities to make a difference?

a. _____

b. _____

c. _____

d. _____

e. _____

Your Opportunities

Some opportunities are just thrust upon you. You almost have no choice, or so it seems. But also look at how you spend your time, some of which is "survival" time: time you need to spend doing your job to keep it; to keep connected to your spouse, significant other, family, or friends or else you will lose them; to complete a task that, if you don't do it, someone or something will suffer and you will lose the opportunity or money or self-respect. This is time that tends to grab your attention. It could be something simple; for example, if you don't move the furniture out of the room this morning, the painters won't paint your room this afternoon, or if you don't write and send in the details of your proposal to a potential client by 3 p.m. on Friday, you will not be considered for the contract.

Most of this time spent is probably necessary. But some of it may be a matter of perspective, and you may be able to save some of that time to make a difference in other ways by using your planning or negotiation skills or other time management strategies. Research by Kahneman et al. (2006) indicates that time use may be one of the most important determinants of a sense of well-being and the factor that we can most improve upon. Look at the percentage of time you spend "killing" versus the time you are dedicating on a regular basis to making a difference. Decide what percentage of your time you want to "kill" next week and what percentage you want to dedicate to using your abilities and motivation to make a difference at work and in your relationships. Use exercise 16 to examine and choose potential opportunities to make a difference.

EXERCISE 16

Your Opportunities to Make a Difference

1. Situations at work. Review your work schedule for next week. Think about who you will be working with and what tasks you will be undertaking. Identify several specific opportunities where you will attempt to use your core personality type to make a difference. Describe those opportunities below and then circle the one you are most committed to fulfilling.

_____

_____

_____

_____

_____

_____

_____

_____

_____

continues

Exercise 16 cont'd

2. Situations in relationships. Think about the week ahead of you. Identify specific relationships (e.g., with your significant other, spouse, friends, neighbors, etc.) in which you could attempt to use your natural abilities to make a difference. Describe the individuals/relationships below and then circle the one you are most committed to engaging.

_____

_____

_____

_____

_____

_____

_____

_____

_____

_____

MAKING A DIFFERENCE IN THE SHORT TERM

How are you going to use your natural abilities and motivations to make a difference in the specific work and relationship situations you identified in exercise 16? Exercises 17 and 18, which ask you to outline your short-term plans for this week, can help you begin to develop the habit of making a difference more frequently. Remember that small things can make a big difference. What are you going to do with whom by when and how? Spell out the details of how you will approach the work situations and relationships with the specific steps you will take. How will your personality make you a "natural" in your efforts to make a difference? Apply what you have learned from the previous chapters. Utilize the relevant ideas you gained from the stories of people similar to your personality type. Don't just wait for something to happen— have a plan for making a difference at work and in relationships this week. However, allow yourself to make adjustments to your plans as situations evolve.

EXERCISE 17

Your Short-Term Plan to Make a Difference at Work This Week

What should you do in advance to prepare yourself to make a difference in the specific work situation you identified in step 1 of exercise 16?

_____

_____

_____

_____

How will you approach the situation? Is this something you will do on your own, or will you have to recruit one or more other people to initiate this effort to make a difference? What will you say or do? Be sure your words and actions are consistent with your natural abilities, especially those related to your core personality type as described in chapters 4–7. Capitalize on your motivation to make a difference, too. You may want to practice your opening lines or review your plan of initiating action with a trusted friend or colleague before you take the action. Consider using the feedback you receive from this person to enhance your first step.

_____

_____

continues

Exercise 17 cont'd

_____

_____

_____

_____

_____

_____

Spell out any other details you can anticipate about how you will use your abilities and motivation to make a difference in the situation you selected.

Behaviors or abilities you will engage in order to make a difference in this situation:

_____

_____

_____

_____

_____

_____

Steps you will take (what you will do with whom by when and how):

_____

_____

_____

_____

_____

_____

EXERCISE 18

Your Short-Term Plan to Make a Difference in a Relationship This Week

What should you do in advance to prepare yourself to make a difference in the specific relationship situation you circled in step 2 of exercise 16?

_____

_____

_____

_____

_____

_____

_____

_____

How will you approach this person? Is there anything you need to arrange before your encounter? What will you say or do? Be sure your words and actions are consistent with your natural abilities, especially those related to your core personality type as described in chapters 4–7. Capitalize on your motivation to make a difference, too. You may want to practice your opening lines or review your plan of initiating action with a trusted friend or colleague before you initiate the contact. Consider using the feedback you receive from this person to enhance your first step.

_____

_____

_____

_____

_____

continues

Exercise 18 cont'd

_____

_____

_____

Spell out any other details you can anticipate about how you will use your abilities and motivation to make a difference in the relationship you selected.

Behaviors or abilities you will engage in order to make a difference in this relationship:

_____

_____

_____

_____

_____

_____

Steps you will take (what you will do with whom by when and how):

_____

_____

_____

_____

_____

_____

_____

_____

_____

_____

LESSONS LEARNED

In exercises 17 and 18, you planned how you would make a difference during one week, both at work and in a relationship. How did things go? Were you able to use your natural abilities and motivations associated with your core personality type? Exercise 19 will help you examine what you learned from those efforts.

EXERCISE 19

Lessons Learned from Last Week's Efforts

You were asked to attempt to use your natural abilities and motivations to make a difference in a specific situation at work and in a relationship. Simply describe what actually happened, without trying to evaluate it.

_____

_____

_____

_____

_____

To what extent did you use the natural abilities associated with your core personality type (Stabilizer, Harmonizer, Catalyst, or Visionary) in the effort? Was your motivation to make a difference reinforced?

_____

_____

_____

_____

_____

_____

continues

Exercise 19 cont'd

What did you learn or relearn in the effort to make a difference at work? How could you make use of what you learned in a future situation at work?

_____

_____

_____

_____

_____

_____

What did you learn or relearn in the effort to make a difference in a relationship? How could you make use of what you learned in a future relationship?

_____

_____

_____

_____

_____

_____

MAKING A DIFFERENCE OVER THE LONG TERM

William James (2007) suggested that it takes twenty-one days to form a new habit. Loehr and Schwartz (2004) estimate that most activities become a habit in one month. Repeat the exercises in this chapter for at least the next three to four weeks. Make them part of your weekly routine. Learn from your efforts to use your core personality type to make a difference.

Now examine what you could do to make a difference at work and in relationships more frequently over the next year. What could you do to live your life more consciously? What aspects of your personality, abilities, and motivation do you want to keep in the forefront of your mind as you go forward? What will you do to more readily recognize opportunities to make a difference at work and in your relationships? What lessons have you learned or relearned from reading this book that will enhance your efforts to live a life that makes a difference more frequently? How will you apply what you have learned? Completing exercise 20 will help you in your efforts.

EXERCISE 20

Living Your Life More Consciously

1. What lessons have you learned about how you could more frequently make a difference at work by using your personality, abilities, and motivation? Be specific. (Add more lessons if appropriate.)

a. _____

_____

_____

b. _____

_____

_____

c. _____

_____

_____

Exercise 20 cont'd

2. What lessons have you learned about how you could more frequently make a difference in your relationships by using your personality, abilities, and motivation? Be specific.

a. _____

_____

_____

b. _____

_____

_____

c. _____

_____

_____

3. How could you make use of what you learned? What longer-term plans could you make to apply the lessons you have learned? What are you willing to do to reward yourself for making and implementing these plans?

_____

_____

_____

_____

_____

_____

_____

_____

_____

SUMMARY

It is in our best interest to attempt to make a difference in life, and if we all tried to do that more often, the world would be a better place, too. You have been born with some natural abilities and have developed some others in your lifetime. These strengths of your personality type form the basis of how you can contribute by being yourself. It is my hope that you are now more aware of the ways you can use your personality at work and in relationships. If you completed the exercises in this book, you will have examined your abilities, motivations, and opportunities to do so. How are you unleashing the Stabilizer, Harmonizer, Catalyst, or Visionary in you? Let's personalize this national/international movement toward making a difference. How are you making a difference by being yourself, by putting your core personality type to good use? Feel free to contact me through my Web site, www.makingadifferencetype.com, with your stories and adventures. Together we can make many differences in our own different ways.

VERIFYING YOUR MBTI®
PERSONALITY TYPE

If you have identified your four-letter type using the MBTI instrument or the "Quick Estimate" exercises in this book, you can use the charts on the following four pages to check whether you still think those four preferences describe your "best-fit" type. On each chart are two columns, one for each preference of a preference pair. You will probably see items that describe you in both columns, but try to determine which column is more consistent with the way you are when you are being yourself. Remember, situations drive behaviors—from time to time we all are capable of acting in many different ways to match the needs of a given situation. Which column is most in line with the real you?

After reviewing the charts, which do you believe
to be your true preferences?

E or I	S or N	T or F	J or P

Life Orientation Preferences: Energy

EXTRAVERSION (E)

Those with a preference for Extraversion tend to:

1. Be outwardly directed
2. Be action oriented: do, consider, do
3. Think out loud to people
4. Gain energy by interacting
5. Be willing to "wing it"—learn by trial and error
6. Be more accessible; others understand them better
7. Have broad interests
8. Sometimes view things superficially
9. Be more optimistic
10. Perceive and respond to external, informal standards
11. Enjoy working with others
12. Need isolation to bring out their Introversion
13. Have relationships with many people; be good at starting relationships
14. Focus on the external world of people and things
15. Notice everything; not mind interruptions much
16. Be willing to share what they think and feel
17. Display emotions as they experience them

INTROVERSION (I)

Those with a preference for Introversion tend to:

1. Be inwardly directed
2. Be reflection oriented: consider, do, consider
3. Think a lot before talking
4. Discharge energy by interacting with people; need alone time to recharge
5. Be reserved initially—cautious before acting
6. Be known well by few; may appear more secretive
7. Have deep interests
8. Sometimes appear intense
9. Be resistant to generalizations
10. Not pick up on norms or ignore them; set their own standards
11. Enjoy working alone
12. Need structure and a defined role to bring out their Extraversion
13. Limit their number of relationships; find small talk and first steps of a relationship difficult, though are loyal in established relationships
14. Focus on the internal world of ideas and experiences
15. Hate to be interrupted; are more comfortable with silence
16. Wait to be asked about what they think or feel
17. Bottle up emotions

Perceiving Function Preferences: Taking In Information

SENSING (S)

Those with a preference for Sensing tend to:

1. Be more interested in facts and actualities
2. Attend to details; see the trees more than the forest
3. Depend on the five senses—very aware of physical surroundings
4. Be more patient with routines
5. Be sensible, practical, pragmatic, down-to-earth
6. Be present oriented; see what is and be likely to be content with it
7. Hate to see things made overly complicated
8. Be steady workers
9. Be systematic and persistent
10. Mistrust intuition
11. Have and value common sense
12. Be investigators and implementers
13. Learn by imitating and through instruction
14. Be better at responding to what is actually said
15. Require experiencing something through their senses to really understand it
16. Believe creativity is 99 percent perspiration and 1 percent inspiration

INTUITION (N)

Those with a preference for Intuition tend to:

1. Be more interested in possibilities
2. Notice the patterns; see the forest more than the trees
3. Depend on intuition—independent of physical surroundings
4. Be more patient with complexity
5. Be imaginative, innovative, and idealistic; have head in the clouds
6. Future oriented; see what could be and often be restless for change
7. Enjoy complexity and theories
8. Work in bursts
9. Jump to conclusions
10. Ignore some facts
11. Have and value creativity
12. Be originators, promoters
13. Learn by initiating and insight
14. Read between the lines
15. Understand many things through gut feelings and hunches
16. Believe that creativity comes in flashes of inspiration

Judging Function Preferences: Making Decisions

THINKING (T)

Those with a preference for Thinking tend to:

1. Apply principles of logic to reach conclusions
2. Emphasize an objective, true–false orientation
3. Sometimes come across as impersonal without intending to be
4. Be analytical, skeptical, and questioning
5. Choose truth over tact
6. Appreciate a good argument
7. Feel justice = treating everyone the same
8. Be very concerned with fairness
9. Systematically apply policies and laws in making decisions about people
10. Persuade via logic
11. Be more likely to rationalize their values and beliefs
12. Take good work (own and others) for granted
13. Be less likely to be sensitive to feelings—their own or others'
14. Examine consequences from an objective point of view
15. Be more likely to intellectualize their feelings
16. Contribute to problem solving by exposing flaws to solutions and through systematic analysis

FEELING (F)

Those with a preference for Feeling tend to:

1. Apply values and beliefs to reach conclusions
2. Emphasize a subjective, agree–disagree orientation
3. Be more naturally friendly unless values are threatened
4. Be more trusting, sometimes overly accepting
5. Choose tact over truth
6. Fear conflict; prize harmony
7. Feel justice = treating all people as individuals
8. Treat others as they would like to be treated
9. Do what seems "right" in situations involving people
10. Persuade by appealing to values and arousing enthusiasm
11. Clearly know their priorities, beliefs, and values
12. Give and desire appreciation readily
13. Be more likely to be able to predict their own and others' feelings
14. Examine consequences from a subjective, "people" point of view
15. Be more likely to think subjectively
16. Contribute to problem solving by encouraging others and establishing ethical guidelines for making decisions

Attitude Function Preferences: External World

JUDGING (J)

**Those with a preference
for Judging tend to:**

1. Push for closure
2. Keep plugging away until the job is finished
3. Get the most pleasure from finishing things
4. Be more decisive and purposeful
5. Push for decisions too quickly
6. Prefer a planned and orderly approach; need certainty
7. Like schedules and to-do lists, and try to fulfill them
8. Want things decided in advance with expectations made clear
9. Be more self-disciplined
10. Be more goal and outcome oriented
11. Want to know only the best way to do things
12. Rigidly follow plans sometimes
13. Take deadlines seriously
14. Be more likely to set standards for self and others and have defined opinions
15. Cut off information too quickly to reach a wise decision sometimes
16. Favor their T–F function over their S–N function
17. Feel anxious until a decision is made, but then relax

PERCEIVING (P)

**Those with a preference
for Perceiving tend to:**

1. Push for understanding
2. Keep things open-ended; hate to miss out on anything
3. Get the most pleasure from starting things
4. Be more flexible and indecisive but better at generating options
5. Put off decisions too often
6. Prefer a spontaneous approach; more tolerant of ambiguity
7. Like to respond to things as they arise
8. Want to keep options open
9. Be more easily distracted
10. Be more process oriented
11. Want to know all the ways to do things
12. Fail to follow through sometimes
13. Take deadlines as a starting point
14. See both sides of an argument; be more tolerant; hold more tentative opinions
15. Seek out more information than they need or could use sometimes
16. Favor their S–N function over their T–F function
17. Be anxious before a decision, and then prone to second-guessing

Source: Adapted from Gregory E. Huszczo, *Tools for Team Excellence* (Mountain View, CA: Davies-Black Publishing, 1996), tables 11–14, pp. 141–147.

YOUR CORE PERSONALITY TYPE AT WORK

You can use the following exercise to quickly estimate your core personality type as it manifests itself at work.

Think about how your personality tends to manifest itself at work. What are you like when you are being yourself at work? Items A–M are each followed by a set of choices. Rank order each set from 1 to 4, where:

1 = Most like the real you
2 = More like you than the other choices but not as much as 1
3 = Somewhat like you but relatively less than 1 or 2
4 = Somewhat like you but less like you than any other choice

A. Words that best describe you on teams and when you have to make decisions:

_____ Practical and matter-of-fact (ST)

_____ Sympathetic and friendly (SF)

_____ Enthusiastic and insightful (NF)

_____ Logical and ingenious (NT)

B: What you want from others when seeking coaching/advice:

_____ Honesty (ST)

_____ Personal knowledge about you (SF)

_____ Unique treatment (NF)

_____ Businesslike demeanor, at least at first (NT)

continues

C. What you want when dealing with a salesperson:

_____ The facts—specifics and logical implications of the specifics (ST)

_____ Personalized service—especially about the kind of people who like the product or service (SF)

_____ An idea of their vision—the big picture and impact of the product or service on people and their values (NF)

_____ Logical options—especially how the possibilities create systems and frameworks (NT)

D. What you use in your basic approach to problem solving and decision making:

_____ Facts derived from impersonal analysis, and technical skills in facts and objective things (ST)

_____ Facts from a personal analysis, and practical help and services for people (SF)

_____ Possibilities from a personal analysis, and understanding and communicating with people (NF)

_____ Possibilities from an impersonal analysis, and logical but ingenious theoretical development of ideas (NT)

E. Your preferred organizational strategy:

_____ Is detailed, practical, sensible; takes an "If it ain't broke, don't fix it" approach; introduces changes on a trial basis; is patient; provides full documentation; focuses on one step at a time; examines physical features of work setting; is economical (ST)

_____ Emphasizes values; is down-to-earth but caring; is present oriented; is based on experience; considers personal reactions; seeks immediate results (SF)

continues

_____ Is innovative and creative; takes risks to promote values; sells the strategy; provides multiple options; emphasizes development and relationships; is based on values; is future and people oriented (NF)

_____ Considers the big picture; is future and goal oriented; is innovative; uses theories or frameworks; takes calculated risks; formulates more than executes plans (NT)

F. Your preferred organizational structure:

_____ Is logical and organized; is hierarchical and centralized, maybe even bureaucratic; provides clear channels; uses checks and balances to reduce risks; has legalistic job descriptions (ST)

_____ Is all one big family; provides many channels for input; has clear but fair expectations; keeps everyone together (SF)

_____ Is loose and organic; functions as an adhocracy: flat and decentralized; has growth-oriented job descriptions (NF)

_____ Is complex, decentralized, and rational; provides just enough structure to encourage productivity (NT)

G. Your preferred organizational systems/procedures:

_____ Are clear; follow routines; use formats for reports; include systematic data gathering and formulas for decisions; rely on hard data and experience; emphasize schedule and costs, control and certainty; say, "Show me" (ST)

_____ Produce routines that feel good; use formats for reports but expect personal perspectives to be included; allow vast input; gather facts, details, opinions, examples, and reactions from people—not through impersonal means; review what has worked before (SF)

_____ Are flexible and unstructured; expedite communications; allow for personal judgments and hunches; include brainstorming sessions to discover alternatives (NF)

continues

Exercise cont'd

_____ Are flexible in format but rational in content; use processes that expedite the examination of ideas; are results, not procedures, oriented; gather information fast and use it to gain a sense of progress; show the connections between the parts; are integrative (NT)

H. Your preferred leadership style:

_____ Emphasizes dependability and fairness; is oriented toward details and facts; stresses developing and then following plans; tends toward bluntness, reinforcing compliance, objectivity, and accountability; is matter-of-fact, down-to-earth, and impersonal (ST)

_____ Emphasizes being people oriented, considerate, compassionate, fair, dependable, tolerant, participative, supportive, and practical; makes sure all have their say; demonstrates live-and-let-live attitude; resolves conflict through compromise and/or accommodation (SF)

_____ Emphasizes being willing to sacrifice for the greater good; tends to be participative, democratic, charismatic, dramatic, idealistic, enthusiastic, appreciative, sociable, and personable; is manifested in high-energy bursts; shows desire to rescue others; is evolutionary; smooths over conflicts; leaves decisions open to modification (NF)

_____ Emphasizes being open to intriguing and far-reaching possibilities; is confident, revolutionary, blunt, and impersonal; shows ability to provide meaning, asks "Why?"; emphasizes debate, ideas, progress, and breakthroughs (NT)

I. Your preferred approach to treating staff:

_____ Involves categorizing employees, using clear selection criteria for each job, hiring people who respond to rules and regulations; admires common sense; does not emphasize self-awareness; respects tough-minded people who can get others to do their job; emphasizes work roles more than workers (ST)

continues

Exercise cont'd

_____ Shows concern for whether people feel they belong; socializes/molds people toward company values; emphasizes training and development opportunities, sharing the work load equitably, not criticizing people publicly, and putting workers before work roles; facilitates interaction between members; seeks personal testimonials (SF)

_____ Pushes development and use of potential; includes selecting people who fit in; finds the good in all; values fun, encourages insight and search for meaning, enhances relationships, and motivates and excites others (NF)

_____ Utilizes executors; pushes high expectations; demands competency; is responsive to new ideas; fosters impersonal relationships with a focus on accomplishment (NT)

J. Your preferred skills:

_____ Absorbing and using details and facts about things; measuring progress; following routines; fixing things; being efficient in meetings and reports (ST)

_____ Absorbing and using details and facts about people; focusing on human resources/services/development/marketing; interpersonal skills; understanding people's routines (SF)

_____ Focusing on customer service and public relations; communicating; showing empathy; having ability to see both sides of issues (NF)

_____ Engaging in R&D; being logical and efficient; planning strategically; integrating systems; problem solving (NT)

K. Your preferred values to promote:

_____ Stability, dependability, orderliness, being realistic, practicality, punctuality, fairness, objectivity, competitiveness, efficiency, security, not rocking the boat (ST)

continues

Exercise cont'd

_____ Affiliation, fairness, proper behavior, respect, trust, loyalty, harmony, pragmatism, the golden rule, anyone can succeed, traditions, cooperation, familiarity, providing a warm workplace where people like to come to work (SF)

_____ Having fun; belief that people are good and important; harmony, cooperation, loyalty, creativity, development, stimulation, variety, autonomy, authenticity, insightfulness, credibility (NF)

_____ Belief in change, profound/complex views, competency, innovation, nonconformity, logic, need for achievement, ingenuity (NT)

L. Weaknesses you may be likely to have as a leader:

_____ Treating strategy as an end, not a means; overguarding against catastrophe, missing the forest for the trees; being too impersonal and matter-of-fact; imposing rigid and legalistic structures, which can make change difficult; compartmentalizing, leading to overspecialization; overrelying on formulas for decision making; nitpicking; resisting innovation; being impatient with complexity; forgetting to appreciate people; taking staff for granted; having difficulty dealing with uncertainty; adhering rigidly to plans; being shortsighted (ST)

_____ Being overconcerned with people; perpetuating positions beyond their usefulness; oversimplifying problems; nitpicking; avoiding conflict; believing solely in hard work; being shortsighted; being softhearted; being a busybody, trying to please everybody, appearing to play favorites; being uncomfortable with complex or abstract situations, passive-aggressive, or self-righteous; missing the forest for the trees (SF)

_____ Having a high need for approval, being a poor disciplinarian; being emotional/dramatic, moralistic, overtrusting, naïve, too flexible, too talkative, inconsistent, late for deadlines, too influenced by personal likes/dislikes; getting overextended; creating dependencies; avoiding conflict; working in bursts; overemphasizing enthusiasm; being poor at details and follow-through; having too many direct reports; reinventing the wheel; trying to rescue lost souls (NF)

continues

_____ Losing interest once things are figured out; lacking follow-through; forgetting to stroke others but needing strokes; being elitist, restless, argumentative, confrontational, critical, impatient with details/routines and repeated mistakes, poor at delegating; spending too much time planning; failing to install clear structures; having weak administrative skills; escalating standards; promoting change for the sake of change (NT)

M. Method of persuasion that is more likely to be successful with you:

_____ (ST)
- Show me that it works
- Indicate how it saves time and money
- Demonstrate a good cost-to-benefit ratio
- Show how the results can be measured
- Allow me to try it before I buy it
- Offer specific applications and benefits
- Answer all my questions

_____ (SF)
- Show me how it will benefit me and those I care about
- Indicate the practical results for people
- Use personal testimonies from those who have benefited from it
- Show that it provides immediate results
- Set it in a personal context
- Show respect to me and others in your presentation

_____ (NF)
- Show me how it will enhance relationships
- State how it will help people grow and develop
- Focus on my own and others' giftedness
- Show how it gives new insights and perspectives
- Indicate that people will like it and, by implication, will like me
- Point out how it will help me find meaning
- Say it's enjoyable and fun

continues

Exercise cont'd

_____ (NT)
- Discuss its research base
- Highlight its theoretical background
- Demonstrate how it fits a strategy
- Show how it will increase competency
- Indicate its broad and far-reaching possibilities
- Show that it has intriguing and fascinating possibilities
- Be a credible source of information

Scoring:

Rankings

Item	ST	SF	NF	NT
A.	____	____	____	____
B.	____	____	____	____
C.	____	____	____	____
D.	____	____	____	____
E.	____	____	____	____
F.	____	____	____	____
G.	____	____	____	____
H.	____	____	____	____
I.	____	____	____	____
J.	____	____	____	____
K.	____	____	____	____
L.	____	____	____	____
M.	____	____	____	____
Total:	____	____	____	____
Average: (Total/13)	____	____	____	____

Source: Adapted from Gregory E. Huszczo, *Tools for Team Leadership* (Mountain View, CA: Davies-Black Publishing, 2004), tables 4–7, pp. 50–58.

Appendix C

"MAKING A DIFFERENCE" THEMES BY CORE PERSONALITY TYPE

Following are lists of themes of the stories from chapters 4–7 illustrating how each core personality type can make a difference at work and in relationships. Use it to remind yourself how you can use your natural preferences to make a difference.

Stabilizers (STs)	
AT WORK	**IN RELATIONSHIPS**
Simplifying things	Doing tasks to be helpful
Getting it done	Being dependable
Moving one step at a time	Enforcing rules
Catching and correcting mistakes	Urging caution/responsibility
Just getting to work	Dealing with reality
Being dependable	Identifying mistakes
Establishing accountability	Improving through small steps
Documenting procedures and information	Compiling things
Enforcing rules and policies	Providing proof
Providing task-oriented training	Encouraging physical activities

Harmonizers (SFs)

AT WORK	IN RELATIONSHIPS
Being there for others	Being there for others
Being positive	Offering encouragement
Being inclusive	Verbalizing feelings
Getting to know others personally	Being loyal
Being respectful, behaving properly	Making others happy
Smoothing conflict	Rescuing others
Showing loyalty to the organization	Hosting
Rescuing individuals	Smoothing conflict
Providing comfort	Advocating values
Creating order	Sacrificing for others

Catalysts (NFs)

AT WORK	IN RELATIONSHIPS
Reaching dreams	Being deeply emotional
Seeing good in everyone	Advocating for causes
Facilitating communication	Creating fun
Rescuing groups of people	Helping others with their relationships
Developing people's potential	Encouraging others to take risks
Developing belief/value systems	Being inspirational
Promoting change through relationships	Using communication skills
Being creative	Growing in relationships
Providing inspirational motivation	Showing empathy, not just sympathy
Helping people understand	Searching for the meaning of life

Visionaries (NTs)	
AT WORK	**IN RELATIONSHIPS**
Utilizing competencies	Making a personal difference impersonally
Challenging self and others	Problem solving and planning
Being an architect of the future	Encouraging independence and self-reliance
Taking charge of change efforts	Helping others increase their competence
Applying knowledge	Using relationship skills learned formally
Motivating others by setting high standards	Using high standards to motivate others
Solving problems with long-term fixes	Negotiating conflicts
Giving expert advice	Using logic in clever ways
Looking at the big picture	Giving and using expertise
Mediating disputes	Taking a big-picture view

REFERENCES

Association for Psychological Type, www.aptinternational.org/

Ben-Shahar, T. 2007. *Happier: Learn the Secrets to Daily Joy and Lasting Fulfillment.* New York: McGraw-Hill.

Buckingham, M. 2007. *Go Put Your Strengths to Work: Six Powerful Steps to Achieve Outstanding Performance.* New York: Free Press.

Buckingham, M., and D. O. Clinton. 2001. *Now, Discover Your Strengths: How to Develop Your Talents and Those of the People You Manage.* New York: Free Press.

Cooperrider, D., and S. Srivastva. 1987. "Appreciative Inquiry in Organizational Life," in *Research in Organizational Change and Development,* vol. 1, eds. R. Woodman and W. Pasmore. Greenwich, CT: JAI Press.

Csikszentmihályi, M. 1990. *Flow: The Psychology of Optimal Experience.* New York: Harper & Row.

———. 2003. *Good Business: Leadership, Flow, and the Making of Meaning.* New York: Simon & Schuster.

Ellis, A., and R. A. Harper. 1974. *A Guide to Rational Living.* Hollywood, CA: Wilshire Book Co.

Gardenswartz, L., and A. Rowe. 1994. *Diverse Teams at Work: Capitalizing on the Power of Diversity.* New York: McGraw-Hill.

George, J. M. 1991. "State or Trait: Effects of Positive Mood on Prosocial Behaviors at Work," *Journal of Applied Psychology* 76, 299–307.

Gladwell, M. 2000. *The Tipping Point: How Little Things Can Make a Big Difference.* New York: Little, Brown & Co.

Glasser, W. 1998. *Choice Theory: A New Psychology of Personal Freedom.* New York: HarperCollins.

Greenleaf, R. 1977. *Servant Leadership: A Journey into the Nature of Legitimate Power and Greatness.* New York: Paulist Press.

Hammer, A. 2007. *The MBTI®Complete: Form M.* Mountain View, CA: CPP, Inc.

Hirsh, S. K., and J. A. G. Kise. 2000. *Introduction to Type® and Coaching.* Mountain View, CA: CPP, Inc.

Horney, K. 1950. *Neurosis and Human Growth.* New York: W. W. Norton & Co.

Huszczo, G. E. 1996. *Tools for Team Effectiveness.* Mountain View, CA: Davies-Black Publishing.

———. 2004. *Tools for Team Leadership.* Mountain View, CA: Davies-Black Publishing.

———. 2006. "Making a Difference at Work," *Bulletin of Psychological Type* 29, 2:25–26.

———. 2007. "Making a Difference and the Influence of Type." Paper presented at the XVII Biannual International Meeting of the Association for Psychological Type, Baltimore, MD (July).

Huszczo, G. E., and G. Bensch, G. 2005. "How Type Influences the Way We Make a Difference in Relationships." Paper presented at the XVI Biannual International Meeting of the Association for Psychological Type, Portland, OR (July).

Huszczo, G. E., and R. Opland. 2004. "Making a Difference: How Type Influences Perceived Contributions at Work." Paper presented at the Biannual International Meeting of the Association for Psychological Type, Toronto, ON (July).

Isen, A. M., M. Clark, and M. F. Schwartz. 1976. "Duration of the Effect of Good Mood on Helping: Footprints on the Sands of Time," *Journal of Personality and Social Psychology* 34, 385–393.

James, W. 2007. *Pragmatism, a New Name of Some Old Ways of Thinking: Popular Lectures on Philosophy.* Longmans, Green, & Co.

Jung, C. G. 1955. *Modern Man in Search of a Soul.* New York: Harvest.

———. 1971. "Psychological Types," in *Collected Works,* vol. 6. Trans. R. F. C. Hull. Princeton, NJ: Princeton University Press.

Kahneman, D., A. B. Krueger, D. Schkade, N. Schwartz, and A. A. Stone. 2006. "Would You Be Happier If You Were Richer? A Focusing Illusion," *Science* 312, 1908–1910.

Kelly, H. H. 1972. "Attributions in Social Interaction," in E. E. Jones, D. E. Kanouse, H. H. Kelly, R. E. Nisbett, S. Vallins, and B. Weiner (eds.), *Attribution: Perceiving the Causes of Behavior* (pp. 1–26). Morristown, NJ: General Learning Press.

———. 1973. "The Processes of Causal Attribution." *American Psychologist* (February): 107–128.

Loehr, J., and Schwartz, T. 2004. *The Power of Full Engagement: Managing Energy, Not Time, Is the Key to High Performance and Personal Time.* New York: Free Press.

Myers, I. B. 1980. *Gifts Differing.* Mountain View, CA: CPP, Inc.

Myers, I. B., with Kirby, L. K., and Myers, K. D. 1998. *Introduction to Type* (6th ed.). Mountain View, CA: CPP, Inc.

Myers, I. B., M. H. McCaulley, N. L. Quenk, and A. L. Hammer. 1998. *MBTI® Manual: A Guide to the Development and Use of the Myers-Briggs Type Indicator®* (3rd ed.). Mountain View, CA: CPP, Inc.

New York Stock Exchange. *People and Productivity.* New York: 1982.

O'Toole, J., and E. Lawler. 2006. *The New American Workplace.* New York: Palgrave Macmillan.

Pearman, R. 1999. *Enhancing Leadership Effectiveness Through Psychological Type.* Gainesville, FL: Center for Applications of Psychological Type.

Peterson, C. 2006. *A Primer in Positive Psychology.* London: Oxford University Press.

Quenk, N. L. 1993. *Beside Ourselves: Our Hidden Personality in Everyday Life.* Mountain View, CA: Davies-Black Publishing.

———. 2002. *Was That Really Me?* Mountain View: Davies-Black Publishing.

Ricard, M. 2006. *Happiness: A Guide to Developing Life's Most Important Skill.* New York: Little, Brown & Co.

Seligman, M. E. P. 2004. *Authentic Happiness: Using the New Positive Psychology to Realize Your Potential for Lasting Fulfillment.* New York: Free Press.

Weiner, B. 1985. *An Attributional Theory of Motivation and Emotion.* New York: Springer-Verlag.

INDEX